William Barnes

Twayne's English Authors Series

Herbert Sussman, Editor

Northeastern University

TEAS 395

WILLIAM BARNES
(1801–1886)
Photograph reproduced from
The Life of William Barnes by Lucy Baxter
(London: Macmillan, 1887).

William Barnes

By James W. Parins

University of Arkansas at Little Rock

Twayne Publishers • Boston

William Barnes

James W. Parins

Copyright © 1984 by G. K. Hall & Company
All Rights Reserved
Published by Twayne Publishers
A Division of G. K. Hall & Company
70 Lincoln Street
Boston, Massachusetts 02111

Book Production by Marne B. Sultz

Book Design by Barbara Anderson

Printed on permanent/durable acid-free
paper and bound in the United States of
America.

**Library of Congress Cataloging
in Publication Data**

Parins, James W.
    William Barnes.

    (Twayne's English authors series ; TEAS 395)
    Bibliography: p. 154
    Includes index.
    1. Barnes, William 1801–1886—Criticism and
interpretation.   2. Dorset in literature.   I. Title.   II. Series.
PR4065.P37 1984   821'.8   83–22760
ISBN 0–8057–6881–5

For Joe and Marian Parins

Contents

About the Author

The author is presently professor of English at the University of Arkansas at Little Rock where he teaches nineteenth-century literature. He formerly served as chairman of the department there, after teaching at the University of Wisconsin–Stevens Point.

He has published articles on Victorian literature and is the coauthor of *Structure and Meaning: An Introduction to Literature.* He is the literary editor of several concordances to the works of Joseph Conrad and to the *Cantos* of Ezra Pound. Recent publications include *A Biobibliography of Native American Writers 1772–1924* and *American Indian and Alaska Native Newspapers and Periodicals 1826–1924,* both with Daniel F. Littlefield, Jr.

The author is a native of Green Bay, Wisconsin, has a degree in history from St. Norbert College, and holds the M.A. and the Ph.D. from the University of Wisconsin–Madison where he worked under Todd K. Bender.

Preface

William Barnes was a country preacher and schoolmaster who seldom strayed from his home in Dorset, the county of his birth. Although almost entirely self-educated, Barnes was a prolific poet, publishing several volumes of verse in both the Dorset dialect and national English. In addition, he carried out linguistics studies, teaching himself scores of languages and writing books on philology and the origin of language. He was a scientist and historian as well, bringing his self-taught knowledge to the public through a series of books and articles.

Barnes was the complete Victorian. His interests ranged from poetry to geology, from the study of Persian literary genres to practical mechanical physics. At a time when biological evolution was a hotly debated subject, Barnes was a pioneer in teaching natural science in his school. While the "condition of England" and the social and economic welfare of her people were matters for grave concern in London, Manchester, and the other great cities, Barnes was home in Dorset writing *Views on Labour and Gold,* his economic and social treatise. As historians like Thomas Carlyle and Thomas Macaulay tried to use the past to explain the present, Barnes conducted archeological digs and consulted ancient documents in search of Britain's Celtic and Saxon heritage. When the Grimms, the Schlegels, and the Furnivalls invented the scientific study of language, Barnes was at the cutting edge of the philological revolution. Although isolated in rural Dorset, he participated in the major intellectual efforts of nineteenth-century England.

But it is as a literary man that Barnes is remembered. His readers and admirers included many other writers and poets of Victorian England, people like Alfred Lord Tennyson, Gerard Manley Hopkins, Thomas Hardy, Coventry Patmore, and Edmund Gosse. Modern appreciations have come from Geoffrey Grigson and E. M. Forster. His dialect poems make good reading for their historical and linguistic interest alone. But his depictions of country life in the Victorian era, its landscapes, its customs, its problems, and its people, make Barnes the poet what one of his reviewers called him—truly a modern classic.

The present study examines the range of Barnes's activities in an attempt to show their interrelatedness. The material is organized into subject areas, and every attempt has been made to show how the various interests influenced and affected one another. It is hoped that this work will add to the understanding of the Victorian intellectual landscape.

James W. Parins

University of Arkansas at Little Rock

Acknowledgments

Acknowledgment is gratefully given to Southern Illinois University Press for permission to use quotations from *The Poems of William Barnes,* edited by Bernard Jones.

Valuable assistance in the typing of the manuscript was given by Vikki Elliot, Rhonda Reagan, and Ellen Camp. Brenda Caudle and Marie Ryan helped by securing necessary interlibrary loans. The work could not have been completed without the assistance and cooperation of my wife, Marylyn Jackson Parins. I thank her for her help.

Chronology

1801   William Barnes born at "Rushay," near Pentbridge in Dorset.

1806–1814   Attends dame school and later grammar school.

1814   Leaves school and goes to work for Solicitor Dashwood.

1818   Leaves Dashwood and goes to Dorchester to work for Lawyer Coombs. Meets Julia Miles, his future wife.

1820   "To Julia" in the *Weekly Entertainer*. Betrothed to Julia Miles.

1823   Becomes master of the school at Mere, in Wiltshire. Begins intensive study of language, taking up Latin, Greek, French, Italian, German, Persian, and Russian.

1827   Marries Julia. Moves into Chantry House.

1829   *The Etymological Glossary.*

1831   Begins study of Welsh.

1833   *The Mnemonic Manual. A Catechism of Government in General, and of England in Particular.*

1835   Moves to Dorchester and sets up boarding school. Appointed secretary of the Dorset County Museum; his interest in geology and archeology grows. *A Mathematical Investigation of the Principle of Hanging Doors, Gates, Swing Bridges, and other Heavy Bodies.*

1840   *An Investigation of the Laws of Case in Language.*

1842   *The Elements of Grammar. The Elements of Linear Perspective and the Projections of Shadows.*

1844   *Poems in the Dorset Dialect.*

1846   *Poems, Partly of Rural Life in National English.*

1847   Ordained a priest. *Outlines of Geography and Ethnography for Youth.*

1847–1850   Studies during vacations at Cambridge.

1849   *Se Gefylsta: An Anglo-Saxon Delectus. Humilis Domus: Some Thoughts on the Abodes, Life, and Social Condition of the Poor, especially in Dorsetshire.*

1850   Receives B.D., Cambridge.

1851   Dorchester Institute (a workingmen's improvement club) founded by Barnes and others.

1852   Julia dies.

1854   *A Philological Grammar.*

1859   *Views of Labour and Gold.*

1861   Receives Civil List pension from Lord Palmerston, ending financial problems. "The Beautiful in Nature and Art." Begins correspondence with Patmore. *Tiw: A View of the Roots and Stems of the English as a Teutonic Language.*

1863   *A Grammar and Glossary of the Dorset Dialect. Third Collection of Poems in the Dorset Dialect.*

1868   *Poems of Rural Life in Common English.*

1869   *Early England and the Saxon-English.*

1870   Involvement with the Somerset Archaeological Society and Dorset Field Club. Continuing interest in archeology and antiquities.

1878   *An Outline of English Speechcraft.*

1879   *An Outline of Redecraft, or Logic.*

1884   Last illness begins with chill in rainstorm. Despite his ailments, he remains alert and active.

1886   Barnes dies.

Chapter One
The Dorset Poet

When William Barnes died in 1886, Thomas Hardy commented, "the world has lost not only a lyric writer of a high order of genius, but probably the most interesting link between present and past forms of rural life that England possessed."[1] This high regard by a fellow Dorsetman was shared by others—Gerald Manley Hopkins, Alfred Lord Tennyson, and Coventry Patmore to name a few. They admired this extraordinary man for his learning, for his sensitivity and taste, and for his sense of history, but most of all for his poetry. The extent of Barnes's interests and expertise would be remarkable in itself but is all the more so because the man received little formal education, and also because he hardly ever ventured very far from his place of birth in the country. Barnes was one of those rare individuals whose learning is at the same time encyclopedic and self-taught; he was a Renaissance man in every sense of the term.

William Barnes was born on 22 February 1801 (although Hardy puts it at 1800) at Rushay farm in the vale of Blackmore, Dorset. Dorset had been the home of his farmer father, John Barnes, and indeed that of the Barnes family for many centuries. Dorset is a county with a mild climate in the southwest of England long known for its agriculture. Part of the land is hilly, being a section of the Western Downs, but much of the county is gently rolling, well-watered, and fertile. Major rivers draining Dorset include the Frome and the Stour, mentioned often in the works of both Barnes and Hardy. The most important geological feature of the land is a formation known as the Chalk; this is a belt of land about twelve miles wide which dominates the center of the region. Many of the clay beds of the area are fossiliferous and contain the remains of large reptiles, while other formations and outcroppings provide geological interest. The history of the area is rich and varied and the landscape is dotted with the remains of past settlements. Roman forts, early English burial mounds, medieval castles and monasteries, along with various primitive cairns and barrows have long been studied in the region. The people of Dorset have long spoken their own dialect, derived from the Saxon, which is easily distinguishable from those of neighboring counties. The country is peaceful and productive, blessed with a mild climate. These pleasant surroundings were to be the poet's home for life, and he seldom strayed from them.

Barnes was fortunate in his parents.[2] His father, John, was a hardworking, honest farmer who instilled in his son a love of the land and of the rural life; his mother, Grace Scott, was a woman of refinement and taste. From early on, she was able to foster in her son a love of art, poetry, and learning which stayed with him throughout his life. Unfortunately, the mother died while Barnes was still quite young; as a result, she was able only to begin her son's journey into learning. Little record of his early education remains. He began at one of the village dames' schools, which were elementary schools kept by schoolmistresses or "dames" who usually provided only the most rudimentary education. Barnes soon began a daily trek to Sturminster, a town near his home, to attend an endowed school. The master at this elementary school, Tommy Mullet, must have had a high opinion of young William, for when in 1814 or 1815 a local solicitor came to Mullet looking for a clerk, the schoolmaster recommended Barnes. Mr. Dashwood, the lawyer, was looking for a boy who could copy deeds and perform other basic legal functions.

His work in the attorney's office seemed to be compatible with his temperment. After hours he occupied his time attending to his education. His intellectual curiosity was impressive, and he soon was noticed by a local clergyman, Mr. Lane Fox, who lent him books, especially the classics, and helped tutor the young scholar in unfamiliar subjects. His lifelong love affair with music was nurtured during this time too, by his association with his organist, a Mr. Spinney. Barnes's life at Sturminster continued in this pleasant manner until 1818 when he left Dashwood's office to work for Mr. Coombs, another lawyer who practiced in Dorchester.

In Dorchester, the town which would become the center of his life, he took an apartment above a pastry shop with another young man, William Carey. Barnes and Carey spent most of their time away from the office reading and studying. At this time, the future poet was fortunate to be able to make the acquaintance of a clergyman named Mr. Richman, rector of St. Peter's, who had a good library, a knowledge of the classics, and was willing to tutor the eager young clerk.

It was during this time that Barnes made another friendship which was to influence his life greatly. Edward Fuller was a young bachelor living in Dorchester who shared Barnes's love of music and language. The two studied French together and also joined in musical duets, Fuller playing the flute and Barnes the violin. Music was to remain a favorite pastime for Barnes for the rest of his life. Edward and William became fast friends and, along with Carey and Richman, were a cadre of students of literature and the arts in Dorchester. It was during this time that the foundations for much of Barnes's poetic practice and linguistic theory were laid.

These years were remarkable for another reason, too; in 1818, shortly after arriving to work for Coombs, Barnes met Julia Miles, the daughter of an excise officer asigned to Dorchester. Later, the poet maintained that it had been love at first sight, and that he had known from the moment he had laid eyes on her that she would become his wife. At any rate, by 1820 his first poem, a love poem entitled "To Julia," was published in the *Weekly Entertainer* indicating that the young bachelor was smitten by Miss Miles soon after their initial meeting. They became engaged in the same year the poem came out.

Barnes published *Poetical Pieces* in Dorchester in 1820, printed several small pieces in the *Weekly Entertainer* in the next two years, and in 1822 brought out *Orra, A Lapland Tale*. The two volumes were brought out with the author acting as publisher and underwriting the costs of printing, a common practice during this time. Twenty-two more years passed before Barnes published another volume of verse, although he did bring out some short poems in the *Dorset County Chronicle* in the intervening period.

In 1823, his friend William Carey learned of a vacancy at his old school at Mere in Wiltshire, a neighboring county. Carey wrote and recommended Barnes for the headmastership. At first the poet was reluctant to leave Dorchester, the center of his life, but soon became convinced that he would be better able to marry Julia on a teacher's salary than he would on a clerk's. Julia, too, approved of the plan. She remained behind in Dorchester when William moved to Mere, the two separating temporarily in order to be able later to live together permanently.

Barnes's life at Mere closely resembled the one he had lately left. Instead of at the law office, he worked at the school, but his leisure time was spent exactly as it was before. He corresponded with Carey in French during this time in order to keep up proficiency in that language while at the same time he began an intensive study of other languages, a study which was to last a lifetime. He took up Latin, Greek, French, and Italian in turn. Russian followed, only to be put aside as a language "lacking in old lore."[3] Persian, too, was taken up at this time, and soon became one of his favorites.

This life as a bachelor scholar-teacher went on for four years until 1827 when Barnes was able to move his school to Chantry House, a large, old-fashioned building which in pre-Reformation days had served as a priest's residence. As soon as he had settled there, he returned to Dorchester for Julia Miles; they were married and returned to Mere. For the next eight years, the couple lived in Chantry House where Barnes continued his studies and continued to teach. Here he began to write sonnets in the manner of Petrarch and in 1829 published his *Etymological Grammar,* the first of his many works on philology. A number of his articles began to appear in the *Gentleman's Magazine* during this period, all with linguistic subjects. In 1831, he visited Wales and began his study of Welsh. This soon led to his interest in the language of the Anglo-Saxons and in the very origins of language. Besides his philological papers, he published a number of articles during this time on archeology and architecture, taking advantage of the rich historical heritage of the region. He also took an interest at Mere in mathematics, publishing on this subject as well. This particular interest was probably brought about, on the one hand, by his pedagogical duties and, on the other, by his acquaintanceship with General Shrapnel, the military engineer who invented the shell that bears his name.

By 1835, Barnes felt drawn again to Dorset; he also thought that he might be able to establish a successful boarding school at Dorchester, thus expanding his educational enterprise. So in June 1835, the family packed up, the schoolmaster settled his accounts at Mere, and the Barneses moved back to Dorchester. Here he established his boarding school, which soon was filled with pupils. Throughout his teaching career, Barnes was an innovative and thorough master. He combined elements of practical science such as bridge-building and electricity with those of English grammar and composition. He wrote his own textbooks on such diverse subjects as perspective and

ethnography and took the whole school on field trips to the countryside in order to study botany and geology. His methods were
successful, too, in that many of his pupils went on to earn the
highest honors in the universities and to become successful in various
professions.

In 1837, Barnes began his studies at St. John's College, Cambridge, as a "ten years' man." Ten years' men belonged to a special
class of students who were granted the degree of bachelor of divinity
after completing certain exercises and after ten years had elapsed
since admission. Barnes finished the course with flying colors; he
seemed to have no difficulty with the material, since he spent much
of the two summers in residence at Cambridge engaged in his
linguistic pursuits.[4]

Around this time he started writing seriously again for publication
in periodicals, most notably the *Gentleman's Magazine,* on a characteristically wide range of subjects. He continued, too, to write
poems in the Dorset dialect which were printed anonymously in the
Dorset County Chronicle. By 1844, the publisher of the *Chronicle,* G.
Simmonds, persuaded Barnes to bring out a volume of the Dorset
poems with Simmond's firm handling the printing. This done,
Barnes traveled to London to make arrangements with John Russell
Smith for the metropolitan sale of the book. Smith was to handle
many of Barnes's subsequent literary affairs. Reaction to the volume
was mixed, but many critics saw the dialect as a stumbling block
to the poetry, even though Barnes had thoughtfully furnished a
glossary with the poems. This complaint perhaps accounts for much
of the poet's lack of popularity. The work did not escape notice,
however, and the Dorset poet, as he came to be known, had many
admirers both in his home area and around the rest of the country.
These admirers included some of the important literary figures of
the Victorian era including Tennyson, Hopkins, Patmore, and Hardy.

Dorsetshire had long been an area of interest to geologists, antiquarians, historians, and archeologists because of its geological
formations, and its Roman and early English ruins and edifices. In
1845, the South Western Railway announced expansion of the line
from London to Dorset. This project electrified the county; geologists and archeologists were excited about anticipated fossil finds
and exposed strata in cuts through the chalk hills while antiquarians
worried about the destruction of Roman roads and yet undiscovered
ancient British barrows. Geology had become extremely important

and popular in England in the 1840s with the publication of Lyell's
Geology in 1830 and Chambers's *Vestiges of the Natural History of the
Creation* in 1844,[5] and, with the discovery of various fossils and rock
formations, the Dorset area was considered to be one of the most
promising for students engaged in these scientific pursuits. The
coming of the railroad and resultant transformation of the topog-
raphy added to the interest; the Dorchester natives realized that
many specimens of various kinds were likely to be unearthed in the
construction and that these should be studied and preserved. To
this end, the Dorset County Museum was established with the local
member of Parliament installed as president and William Barnes as
secretary. A building was found to house the institution, and soon
many types of specimens, from butterflies to fossils, began to come
in. Barnes and several others set to arranging and classifying amid
much enthusiasm. In 1847, Barnes and the museum members worked
hard to save the remains of a Roman camp at Poundbury which the
railroad threatened to cut through and destroy. The preservationists
were mostly successful and the main portion of the camp was saved
by tunneling underneath it. The museum and ancillary affairs were
to occupy Barnes for much of the rest of his life; even when advanced
in age, he loved to tramp around the countryside in search of fossils
and relics.

Poems, Partly of Rural Life, in National English, was published by
Smith in 1846. This volume contains sonnets and lyrics along with
one narrative poem, "Erwin and Linda," which was Barnes's only
attempt in the *Decameron* genre.

After a series of examinations, Barnes was ordained a priest by
the bishop of Salisbury on 28 February 1847 and became the pastor
of Whitcombe, a parish in a tiny village three miles from Dorchester. The parish had been served by a nearby abbey until Henry
VIII established it as a separate parish, stipulating that the curate's
salary be set at thirteen guineas a year. Down through the years the
salary remained the same and the parish withered, until it became
a mere outpost of the larger adjoining parish at Came whose rector
became pastor for both. This was the state of affairs when the pastor
at Came suggested that Whitcombe be given to the newly ordained
Barnes. Meager as the living was, he accepted the new position with
gratitude.

During the summers of 1847 and 1848, while his students were
on vacation, Barnes spent his days at Cambridge completing the

work on his degree. While the degree, which was conferred in October of 1850, was the bachelor of divinity, records show that the books he took from the library to read were almost entirely on philology.[6] Much of this reading prepared him to write his *Philological Grammar*. In the meantime, he brought out his *Anglo-Saxon Delectus* in 1849 with the hope that it would contribute to the study of Old English. The replacement of much of the old language by words derived from Latin and Greek was a great loss, he believed; the poet wanted to make speakers of English aware of the language's heritage, of its origins in Teutonic speech, much of which he thought was unfortunately ignored. Later, much of his attention was given to efforts to "purify" English; that is, he tried to convince people to drop words of "foreign" derivation and to use only those which developed from the Anglo-Saxon language.

During the first half of the nineteenth century, a number of associations known as mechanics' institutes had sprung up all over England. The mechanics' institutes were started originally as a means of educating workmen in the elements of scientific knowledge by providing libraries and lectures by men learned in various areas. The thrust was not to be purely practical, although the main aim of the founders of the movement was to make the members better workers. It was thought that a knowledge of science would do a great deal, too, to make the members more religious and more judicious in their choice of political and social theory. Later, the offerings of the institutes became less narrow and branched out into more literary topics, as Richard Altick tells us in *The English Common Reader*.[7] This change came about for several reasons, but the main one was most probably the need to establish as broad a base of support and attendance as possible. Some of these "literary" lectures covered such topics as "The funeral rites of various nations; the habits and customs of the Eskimos; the life, death, and burial of Mary, Queen of Scots; the games of Greece; the theosophy of India; the sons of Noah; and an inquiry into the esoteric riddle, 'Are the Inhabitants of Persia, India, and China of Japhetic or Shemitic Origin?' "[8]

Not surprisingly, the idea of the broad dissemination of knowledge appealed greatly to Barnes and, with two other clergymen, he founded the Dorchester Institute for just such a purpose. Barnes gave many lectures at the institute and was subsequently called upon to give presentations at other similar associations in the region. In

Sturminster, for example, he lectured on "the Anglo-Saxons, and the founding of the English kingdom, comprising the relation of the Saxons to other Teutonic tribes, with their settlement, institutions, laws, language and literature."[9] The subject is a heady one for workingmen (or anyone else for that matter), but it is a good example of the extent and interrelatedness of Barnes's erudition and interests.

The great loss and sorrow of his life came on 21 June 1852 with the death of his wife after a lengthy illness. His diary, written in Italian, records the shock of the event and the sadness of the days afterward.[10] His solace, he found, was his work, so he turned to the production of his *magnum opus, the Philological Grammar.* He also began to contribute to Russell Smith's new periodical, *Retrospective Review.* Around this time he began painting in watercolors. Since his law clerk days he had engaged in the art of wood engraving and had studied perspective and proportion as parts of his scientific endeavors. It was natural, then, for a poet with these other interests to take up painting; the tendency, too, was no doubt urged by the necessity to keep busy during his time of grief.

By 1853, Barnes had finished his *Philological Grammar,* sending the manuscript to Russell Smith. This work is a universal grammar. That is, Barnes believed that the same laws govern all languages and that these laws can be set forth in a scientific way. Once the science of the common laws which govern all languages is understood, Barnes maintained, it is relatively simple to learn languages which were hitherto unfamiliar. The teaching of this science is the aim of the *Philological Grammar.* In documenting his study, the philologist used examples from some sixty-odd languages, including Romance, Teutonic, Oriental, and American Indian tongues. The preparation which went into the volume was prodigious without doubt, but perhaps the most impressive feature of the grammar is Barnes's insistence on making the study of language scientific. His idea was that language develops and evolves according to natural laws and processes, just as other phenomena do. He set out to discover and codify these laws and processes. In a time when much of philology in England was derivative or impressionistic, Barnes's linguistic work was truly ahead of its time.

During these years, too, Barnes was much occupied with history and archeology. He became friends with Charles Warne of London who at the time was preparing a history of Dorset. Another friend,

Charles Hill of Osmington, was also interested in the antiquities of the region; the three often got together to discuss Roman and British remains. In 1855, Barnes made one of his infrequent trips to London to visit the British Museum and the National Gallery as well as to attend the meeting of the Syro-Egyptian Society. This was a period in which he did a good deal of lecturing, mostly for workingmen's institutes, mostly on history and archeology. By 1856, though, Barnes had begun to give readings of his dialect poems which were well received by listeners from both inside and outside Dorset.

Smith brought out a second set of Barnes's Dorset dialect poems in 1858 entitled *Hwomely Rhymes*. The book was popular in London, so much so that the poet was asked by the Duchess of Sutherland to give a reading to some of his admirers. *Hwomely Rhymes* also seems to have brought Barnes's work to the notice of a French linguist, the Chevalier de Chatelain, who subsequently translated some of them into French. The year 1858, too, saw the publication of *Britain, and the Ancient Britons,* which was well-received and reviewed, but was, like many of Barnes's works, too learned to become a popular success. Here, the poet looks at ancient Welsh literature including the works of Taliesin and the Triads[11] as well as at the legends surrounding Arthur, once again taking issue with some of the current historical thought.

From 1858 until 1861, Barnes underwent some financial difficulties. His two sons were in college and the costs of maintaining them was a burden, especially since he had received little money from his publisher. In all fairness to his publisher, Russell Smith, it must be said that the various publications did not sell very well; Smith, especially when he brought out some of the more esoteric works, was lucky to break even. Barnes had never been wealthy and neither had his family; too, he was not much of a businessman when it came to publishing, preferring to get his work into print without much regard for the market. He usually accepted whatever was offered as payment, being grateful to get his works published. So for a number of reasons, the poet, now passing middle age, found himself and his family financially strapped. It was with immense gratitude and relief, therefore, that he received news from Lord Palmerston that, upon the request of some forty magistrates and members of Parliament, he was the recipient of a seventy-pound annual pension. This was quite an honor, obviously, and demonstrates that while Barnes's works were not best-sellers, they were nonetheless highly regarded by many of his countrymen. The yearly seventy pounds did not make him wealthy, but the pension was enough to help with the expenses of raising his children.

This period, though painful in some regards, was bright in some others. His poetry had attracted the attention of a prominent French dialectician, Prince Lucien Buonaparte, who had been engaged for many years in a comparative study of local dialects. He had collected examples of most of the French and Italian folk ballads and now wanted to add the English. He traveled to Dorchester to meet with Barnes and to enlist his aid in the collecting of the southern dialect versions of the "Song of Solomon." Barnes was happy to oblige; the project led to a long and mutually profitable friendship. During this time, too, the poet was introduced to David Masson, editor of *Macmillan's Magazine,* and later corresponded with Alexander Macmillan himself, who became an admirer of Barnes's work. His first publication in this periodical was his work on aesthetics, "Beauty and Art," published in the May issue of 1861.

The work he called his "hopeful brat" also came out in this important year, although through a common publishing practice of the time, it was dated 1862. This was *Tiw: A View of the Roots and Stems of the English as a Teutonic Language.* Again, this was viewed as an esoteric work hardly decipherable by persons not expert in linguistics; for this reason, it did not enjoy popular appeal. The work is another of Barnes's attempts to codify or at least to make more scientific the study of language.

The year 1862 was also important for the poet, as his financial situation was solidified when he was appointed the rector of Came, a prosperous parish which furnished a comfortable living for its pastor. This appointment once and for all relieved him of money worries and of his dependence on his students for his livelihood. This parish, close to his first church at Winterbourne, was in Barnes's old familiar neighborhood. He looked forward to living out his life ministering to the spiritual needs of his beloved Dorset folk while writing his poetry and carrying out his studies.

In the last twenty years of his life, the poet received homage and appreciations from all over the country. He was considered to be an expert on place names and surnames and received much correspondence with queries on these matters. His fellow poets recognized him too; Coventry Patmore, a popular Victorian poet and thinker, wrote glowing reviews of Barnes's work in widely circulated magazines such as *Macmillan's* and the *North British Review.* Patmore introduced Barnes personally to Tennyson, who had admired the Dorset poems for some time. He also sent the dialect poems to Gerard Manley Hopkins, who admonished his friend Robert Bridges for not taking the pains necessary to enjoy and appreciate Barnes. Presumably, Hopkins was referring to the difficulty with the Dorset speech.

Fellow philologists, too, recognized Barnes's work, but were apparently less appreciative than the poets. Frederick J. Furnivall approached the rector in 1863 asking him to write a paper on the Dorset dialect to be presented to the Philological Society, the major body of linguistics scholars, both amateur and academic, in England. This was done, the paper delivered by Furnivall himself, and the work printed as a part of the transactions of the society. Other works of Barnes's followed, but the members quibbled with his quaint terminology and his insistence on the use of words of Teutonic derivation rather than of those from Latin or Greek. Barnes used the term "matewording" for "synonym," for example, and was greatly chagrined when a grandchild called his toy a "velocipede" rather than a "wheel-saddle."

Barnes's association with the Archaeological Institute began in 1865 when the organization held its annual congress in Dorchester. The poet attended the meeting and, recognized as an expert, was selected as guide to the group. His duties consisted of presiding over caravans which traveled to old castles and abbeys, giving tours of these, and providing information on them. Barnes was well-equipped for the job in every way; his enthusiasm more than made up for any lack of physical strength advancing age might have brought on. Often, his archeological and architectural lectures were interspersed with linguistic lessons as well, especially as they concerned place names. His study of the *Anglo-Saxon Chronicles,* too, served him well in discussing the history of the region.

Poems of Rural Life was published by Macmillan in 1868. This work was written in common English but only after much persuasion by Macmillan and others. Macmillan had printed several of the Dorset poems in his magazine since 1864, and comments from readers about the difficulty of the dialect convinced him that Barnes's verse would be much more popular if written in the common tongue. The volume came out in the United States, too, published in 1869 by Roberts Brothers of Boston and illustrated by Winslow Homer. Some reviews of *Poems of Rural Life* assert that these poems in English are but translations from the Dorset—and indeed, some are—and that the verse loses much in translation. Friends, such as Patmore, agreed, asserting that the refined language was not compatible with the subject matter. In any case, the English poems were not as well-received as the Dorset ones were.

The years 1869 to 1875 were full of scholarship and the pursuit of interests developed earlier. Russell Smith brought out *Early England and the Saxon English* in 1869 in which work Barnes traces the Angles and the Saxons from their origins on the Continent, recounts their conquests in England, and identifies their early settlements. He discusses the Anglo-Saxon religion, laws, customs, and traditions, elaborating on their connections with the Frisians. From this he moved on to a translation of the Psalms, his object being to keep the work as literal as possible while at the same time preserving the traditions of the original language and its literature. The result was successful enough that Barnes's name was submitted to the committee appointed by the Convocation of Canterbury then engaged in revising the Bible. His Psalms were not used, but he was made a corresponding member of the committee.

In 1870, he traveled to London at Charles Tennant's request to give a reading of his Dorset poems to an audience which included Disraeli and other prominent persons. It was on this trip that he met Tennyson and much of London society. Tennant, a member of Parliament, thought much of the rural rector and corresponded with Barnes, surprisingly, not so much on poetry and philology as on social issues such as taxation, paper currency, the franchise, and the Irish question. The grandson of Charles Tennant the wealthy chemical manufacturer, he served in Parliament from 1880 to 1886. He was made a baronet in 1885.[12]

Barnes's American connection began around 1870. In that year, Moncure Conway, an American writer, came to England to meet the Dorset poet. The two, according to an account written by Conway published in the January, 1874, issue of *Harper's Magazine*, spent their time comparing notes on poetry, philology, and folklore; they also discussed the connnections between the English Dorchester and the American town of that name in Massachusetts. The connection between the towns was also a favorite topic of correspondence between Barnes and Daniel Ricketson, another American writer, who exchanged letters with Barnes from about this same time until 1884.

During these years, the poet continued with his historical and archeological studies, taking up in turn a discussion of the derivation of the name "Somerset," a comparative study of Saxon and British churches, the establishment of the Dorset Field Club, and writing a paper on Aethelstan. He also established, through a combination of archeology, philology, and the study of old documents, a complete map of the Roman and pre-Roman road systems. This map and supporting data sought to prove that the British were great road-builders before the Romans entered England. Some of the roads previously thought to be Roman, Barnes asserted, were in fact British, being only used by the Romans later. It is typical for Barnes to bring his knowledge in several branches of learning to bear upon a specific problem in a seemingly unrelated branch.

Barnes took up the sword against the Latinization of English again with the publication of *Speechcraft* in 1878. His "fore-say," or preface, announces that the book is an attempt to purge "derived" words from the language and substitute "pure" ones from the Saxon. Examples of this attempt to purify or "back-word" the language are given in a glossary including the change from "accelerate" to "on-quicken," "alienate" to "unfrienden," "equivalent" to "worth-even-ness." He sought, clearly, to remove the Latin and Greek influence from English, revitalizing it with Teutonic words. For this, a reviewer in *Athenaeum* called him "an enthusiast," which almost goes without saying, but went on to say that his book is valuable inasmuch as it does "do good, as it teaches many overlooked (I [Barnes] say little known) points of speechlore."[13]

By 1874, the two editions of the Dorset poems were out of print and Barnes made a bargain with Kegan Paul to bring out a collected version of the poems in 1878. This was done, with Russell Smith's blessing, and the reviews were excellent. The sales, however, again were limited, the poet, as a result, never receiving much money for his efforts. The recognition, always more important to him, continued as Francis Turner Palgrave, the Oxford Lecturer on Poetry, came to visit from time to time to discuss literature, and as Thomas Hardy brought Edmund Gosse to meet the Dorset poet. Professor John Rhys, Lecturer in Celtic at Oxford, took note of his work in Welsh and other languages and corresponded with Barnes on some items of mutual interest.

Barnes continued to be active even into his eighties. These years saw him ministering to his parishioners, visiting the sick, preaching, traveling mostly on foot even in winter, and always carrying out his pursuit of knowledge. His writing slowed but little in these late years until the very end, and he was still active in the museum and field club. In 1881, the club traveled to Eggardun, an ancient British encampment where Barnes lectured on its history. A wagon was provided for those who found it difficult to walk, but Barnes steadfastly declined to ride. By 1883, though, his health had noticeably declined. It was with difficulty that his children got him to venture far from the house. His old enthusiasm came back momentarily on an excursion to Sturminster, where he had spent his boyhood, but he soon lapsed back again into the rheumatic illness which plagued him. Then, in January 1884, he was caught in a cold winter's rain while walking with Thomas Hardy. Barnes refused an offer of shelter from Hardy, electing to walk home in spite of the weather. Soon after, he had to take to bed with a cold. From that time on, the fatigue, aches, and pains of the illness began to get the best of him. He continued to work as best he could, but he had trouble with moving about much and with writing in particular; the last two years of his life were spent as an invalid. His friends and admirers did not forget him, though, and he continued to receive visitors like Hardy and Gosse. Accolades kept coming, too, such as his election as an honorary member of the Northwestern Literary Society of Sioux City, Iowa. The illness, however, deepened, and at last his heart gave out. The poet died on 11 October 1886.

In spite of his physical isolation from the intellectual capitals of England, William Barnes participated in and contributed to the major movements and discussions of the Victorian period. His knowledge and interests were so broad that he was able to work in a variety of areas and fields including linguistics and language, archeology and geology, traditional and adult education, and social and economic theory—all subjects that fascinated the Victorians.

His work in language and linguistics was well known. In nineteenth-century England, much of the important progress made in philology was made by amateurs rather than by academic or professional linguists. Work on the monumental *Oxford English Dictionary*, for example, was carried out largely by amateur volunteers; the publication of many old and valuable manuscrips came about only through the efforts of literary clubs made up of nonprofessional enthusiasts. Barnes was an amateur in this same tradition, carrying out his research for the sheer joy of acquiring knowledge and imparting it to others.

Amateurs with an avocation made contributions to other areas of learning as well in Victorian England. Many important scientific discoveries were made by self-taught men in search of more knowledge. Scientific clubs abounded, like the Dorset Field Club, which helped, through organized support, push toward the frontiers of science. Museums and other scientific institutions, like the Dorset County Museum, played an important part in the gathering and dissemination of information concerning the study of natural phenomena. Barnes, with his lifelong interest and self-learned expertise in geology, archeology, and paleontology, was caught up in the explosion of popular interest in science that took place in the nineteenth century.

The nineteenth century saw great advances in education, too. Pedagogical issues such as the curriculum of schools—from that of the grammar schools to that of the universities—became objects of public debate and concern. While Englishmen debated as to whether or not to follow the German lead and introduce science and technology to the schools, Barnes went ahead and did it in his own school. He combined science and the liberal arts in his curriculum, often urging his students to use scientific theory or technological practices they had learned as subjects for their composition essays. He did not neglect adult education, either, and, like many of his Victorian counterparts, established and participated in workingmen's institutes in an attempt to bring education to those who had been denied it.

Like Carlyle, Dickens, Macaulay, and Mill, Barnes got caught up in the great debate concerning the "condition of England." He had definite ideas concerning the dignity of labor, the treatment of the poor, and the distribution of wealth. These he brought out in his essays, in a book on economics, and, most eloquently, in his poetry. Thus, in spite of his isolation, Barnes remained in the mainstream of Victorian thought. Because of his interest and erudition in so many areas, it can be said of him that he was the complete Victorian.

Chapter Two

Poetry

The Background

During the eighteenth century much of the cultural attention in Europe was turned toward the classical, toward the rules, standards, and examples codified in ancient Greece and Rome. The cultured European regarded art and architecture, government and society, as well as science and education as being continuations of classical precedents set long ago on the shores of the Mediterranean. The enlightened Englishman, Frenchman, Austrian, or Dane saw, too, that these classical ideals were preserved, fostered, and continued in the great cities, the capitals of the Continent—London, Paris, Vienna, Copenhagen—and that culture radiated from these centers. Progress, they reasoned, depended on the spread of Graeco-Roman based civilization into the hinterlands. A direct corollary of this attitude is the idea that all human endeavor that is not based on the classical tradition is essentially barbarian. Thus all local customs and traditions, vernacular languages and dialects, and folk music and literature were regarded as vulgar by adherents to the neoclassical ideal.

The nineteenth century, with its Gothic revival, its rising emphasis on nationalism, and its antipathy for neoclassical cultural forms and standards, brought a dramatic change in attitude. A new interest in the Gothic, or medieval, civilization brought with it a reexamination of the vernacular languages, most of which evolved from those spoken in the Middle Ages or even earlier. This scholarly interest in linguistics led to the study of medieval and pre-Christian European literature, long ignored by Enlightenment scholars who looked to Roman poets and Greek dramatists instead of to Norse bards and Frankish troubadors. Those studying medieval language and literature soon discovered the links between their subjects and surviving dialects and languages as well as folk legends and ballads. Thus, these extant tongues and tales became important both as instruments for the study of medieval subjects and as objects of scholarly curiosity for themselves.

The rise of nationalism contributed to this interest in vernacular dialects and folklore. National identity became inextricably tied to a national language and a national mythology. Most often, the roots of the national language and literature were to be found in the soil of the outlying districts, not in the paved streets and courtyards of the large cities; thus, the regional dialects and folklore took on a status in the nineteenth century that they had been denied in the eighteenth. This appreciation of regional history is viewed as one of the major aspects of nineteenth-century culture.[1]

The regional interest was widespread and pervasive. Strong for obvious reasons in such emerging states as Germany and Italy, the regional movement was active in many other areas where European civilization was dominant. The Felibrigistes organized in France with the express purpose of restoring and preserving the Provençal language and culture. Similar movements, some less organized than others, sprang up in Denmark, Brittany, Spain, and in Ireland, Scotland, Wales, as well as in various regions of England. Even in the United States melting pot, local writers and artists worked to define and preserve the flavor of various geographical regions.

By these efforts, many languages and dialects have been renovated and popularized for both vernacular and literary use. Folk literature has been revived, too, by the collection and preservation of ballads and legends, music and folklore. In the nineteenth century this happened not only in the rural parts of Europe, but also in the backwoods of the United States and Canada where an impressive effort was undertaken to study the languages and literature of the American Indians.

With the closer study of folk language and literature came the realization that this tradition, while existing independently of the classical current of the literary tradition of a culture, nonetheless has an influence on the "official" tradition. In England, this undercurrent of folk tradition can be found in ballads, songs, nursery rhymes, hymns, and prayers. As cultural historians have pointed out, the songs are often used to accompany labor, and all of the works are inextricably tied to the rural village community.[2] The seasonal rhythm of the agrarian culture is reflected often in these pieces, and traditional village occupations are depicted. Themes center on the rural pattern of life—birth, work, love, more work, and death—and emphasize the values of generations of country folk.

By the beginning of the nineteenth century, however, the traditional pattern of village life was changing because of government policies such as the enclosure system and through that matrix of technological, economic, and social causes and effects which we call the industrial revolution. The enclosure acts did away with the common land each village held, thus removing the major source of sustenance for the farmer who did not own much land. By 1815 most of the lands that were formerly open were enclosed. The acts brought greater prosperity to the farmers who owned larger amounts of land and generally tended to concentrate wealth in the hands of fewer and fewer persons or families. As more and more small farmers were forced to hire out as laborers on the larger land holdings, the wages paid to farmers were driven down. To exacerbate the problem, the industrial revolution introduced agricultural machinery to the farms; from the 1820s on fewer and fewer men were needed to till the land. Many people were forced off the land in this way and were crowded into the cities. Here, too, the labor surplus drove down wages, and those lucky enough to hold a job were forced to work long hours in squalid conditions for little more than subsistance. In a short time, the simple life of the English cottager was transformed.

In the face of these changes, folk language and literature took on a new importance. In some ways they were seen as all that remained of a valued heritage, the last vestiges of a fondly remembered past. To some they were important because they were the repositories of the old values and morals, reflections of a better, more stable world. Those who sought to preserve the folk language and literature were trying to save what was left from the older age; those who used the dialects and tales in writing their own literary works were undoubtedly attempting to re-create that better time, to bring back the golden age.

The Rise of Dialect Literature

The conservation of old dialects and legends by linguists and ethnologists was not the only product of the regionalist phenomenon. Writers all over Europe and North America turned to the language of the common people as a vehicle for their art and to these people themselves as the subject of their art. A good example of such writers is Robert Burns, the Scottish poet who wrote mainly about the people of the rural highlands while using the local vernacular and the popular native verse forms. Far from the unlettered plowman that he was reputed to be, Burns was steeped in the Scottish literary tradition. He took a passionate interest in the songs of the Highlands, especially, and was an avid collector of both the music and the accompanying verse. Many of these verses he revised or rewrote, but for a great number of the old songs he composed entirely new poetry. He collaborated with two famous collectors of native Scottish music, James Johnson and George Thomson, contributing many old and original verses to their anthologies, *Johnson's Scots Musical Museum* (1787–1803) and *Thomson's Select Collection of Original Scotish Airs* (1793–1818). Thus Burns was both a preserver and an originator of vernacular poetry.

John Clare is another example of a poet who grew up close to the rural scenes depicted in his poetry. Clare, the son of a farm laborer in Helpston, Northamptonshire, was a sensitive, delicate young man growing up in a rough rural atmosphere. While his surroundings are not usually considered conducive to the development of poets, young Clare began writing verse at an early age. By the time he was twenty-four, the London publishing firm of Taylor and Hessey brought out two volumes of his poetry, *Poems, Descriptive of Rural Life and Scenery* (1820) and *The Village Minstrel* (1821). The first of these became very popular, admired greatly for its freshness and accuracy. Much of the power of Clare's poetry lies in the fact that he is able to depict country life realistically; much of the effect of this realism is achieved by his use of a rustic diction, a vocabulary dependent at least to some extent on his local Northamptonshire dialect. While Clare is more selective in the use of dialect in his verse than, say, Burns, he nevertheless employs it as an effective tool to achieve a realistic effect.

In the United States, too, various dialects were reproduced in prose and poetry to produce a variety of literary effects. As early as 1704, Sarah Kemble Knight used dialect in her journal to record observations during a trip from Boston to New York. Other American writers, like Washington Irving and James Fenimore Cooper, used vernacular speech for humor and verisimilitude. Later, dialect was employed masterfully by such writers as Mark Twain, who recreated the language of Missouri and other American regions; George

Washington Cable, who recorded Creole speech patterns; Joel Chandler Harris and Thomas Nelson Page, who dealt with black dialect; and James Whitcomb Riley and Bret Harte, who used the language of Indiana and points west. Riley, especially, became famous for his depictions of Indiana natives narrated in the Hoosier dialect. Riley's poetry, like Clare's, was distinctive for a remarkably accurate description of details. He demanded veracity in his own work as well as in the works of others above everything else. In giving advice to an aspiring young poet, Riley says "Never—on penalty of *death!*— must any word not in the vocabulary of the unlettered be used. Their vocabulary must do their thinking, in its place."[3]

This penchant for creating verisimilitude is crucial in the work of all successful dialect writers; all the other reasons for using vernacular language in literature are dependent on this insistence on accuracy. Many times, for example, the reason given for writing in the vernacular is to record a particular dialect, folktale, or ballad before it passes out of existence. Obviously, it is of utmost importance for the recorder to follow Riley's advice and transmit only those sounds, words, and ideas which could have come from the source being used. To do otherwise would be to contaminate, at least to some degree, the product and to compromise its value.

Accuracy is also important when vernacular language is used to provide atmosphere in a literary work, another major reason for its use. Dialect has been used by many writers to make the setting of a piece more realistic, and to give a sense of "local color," as it is called by American literary historians. When Huck Finn's friend Jim says, "Yes; en I's rich now, come to look at it. I owns mysef, en I's wuth eight hund'd dollars. I wisht I had de money, I wouldn' want no mor'," we believe him because the speech is that of an escaped slave. Twain's ear for detail convinces the reader and makes us more willing to suspend our disbelief.

Another reason that writers turn to dialect is to produce humor; vernacular speech has been used for comic effect since at least Chaucer's time. Here again, accuracy is important, especially if the kind of speech being reproduced in the literary piece is familiar to the audience. Great success has been achieved by some American writers in this regard, including one who influenced other writers, George Washington Harris. A good example of Harris's use of dialect speech can be found in his "Parson John Bullen's Lizards." The comment here is made by Sut Lovingood, who has just released a bag of lizards up Parson Bullen's trouser leg, an act which results in the cleric's stripping off his clothes and running naked through the congregation: "Passuns ginerly hev a pow'ful strong holt on wimen; but, hoss, I tell yu thar ain't meny ove em kin run stark nakid over an' thru a crowd ove three hundred wimen an' not injure thar karacters *sum.*" Harris's genius lies in his ability to capture the tone and substance of the country savant who feels compelled to make a universal statement applicable to whichever event happens to be in the public eye at a particular time. The pronouncements of the weed-chewing philosopher add greatly to the humor produced by the slapstick and somewhat crude situation. Humor often depends on true observation; Harris's accurate depiction of Sut Lovingood exploits this idea.

Another reason many writers chose to use vernacular language in their work was that they were following a conscious intention to produce a particular style. Many writers were trying, in Wordsworth's words, "to imitate, and as far as is possible, to adopt the very language of men."[4] In Wordsworth and in others in the nineteenth century, we find a distinct aversion to stilted poetic diction brought about by the eighteenth-century attraction for the stylized phrase and the classical allusion. The use of dialect or of at least a more proletarian or rural vocabulary than their predecessors' led to the development of a particular style among the followers of Wordsworth.

Rising democratic tendencies, too, led to the use of the speech of the common man in literary works. Attitudes toward the lower economic echelons of society were changing in many quarters. The farmer and the rural craftsman, long regarded as necessary but essentially uncultured segments of the population, were coming to be regarded as repositories of wisdom as well as strength. Advances in linguistics and philology showed the peasant to be the data bank for vast quantities of information concerning language and folklore. Too, the industrial revolution had brought significant changes to cities, counties, and whole regions, most often spawning pollution, squalor, and poverty. In the face of these changes, those people who had been able to resist urbanization and to retain their rural lifestyle were idealized and regarded as the remnants of a golden age. Thus their language and folkways took on a new importance to the sometimes envious city dweller. Sympathy for the plight of the poor and a rising social consciousness, too, brought about a change in the way the lower classes were treated in literary works. The depiction of the rustic buffoon one finds in Fielding gives way to the proletarian heroine found in Eliot or Dickens. Vernacular speech, then, often becomes a badge of nobility or innocence in a venal and cynical world; to the Gradgrinds of society, Sissy Jupe's language is abominable, but to the sensitive reader of Dickens's *Hard Times* her words are the music of goodness and common sense.

So the nineteenth century saw the rise of the literary artist steeped in the language and lore of the common man. Hamlin Garland, late in the century, described the literature written by this new artist; "it is the literature of lovers and doers . . . who have not been taught to despise common things. . . . They are rooted in the soil. They stand among the cornfields and they dig in the peat bogs. They concern themselves with modern and very present words and themes, and they have brought a new word, which is to divide in half the domain of beauty."[5] That word—"significance"—demonstrates the artist's concern with the common man and his problems.

Barnes as a Dialect Poet

Barnes established himself as a writer of dialect poetry in 1844 with the publication of *Poems of Rural Life in the Dorset Dialect.* Here he turned to what he knew best for the subject matter of his art— the region and people of Dorset—and used as poetic language for those subjects the only appropriate one—the local dialect. Like Robert Burns, Barnes was an originator and a preserver of local tales and legends. The Dorset poet uses the dialect to produce atmosphere and to enhance the local color of his region as well; his language furnishes his descriptions of the countryside with a fresh point of view. His humor, highlighted with quaint expressions, pokes gentle fun at the foibles and vanities of the country folk. Appropriately enough, Barnes's style is low-keyed and folksy, due in large measure to his use of the rural speech patterns. The use of the Dorset language, too, makes poignant his depictions of country people suffering from unjust social and economic conditions and policies.

The decision to write in the dialect was appropriate for Barnes for other reasons as well. His deep interest in antiquarianism, natural philosophy, and philology doubtless played a major part. Barnes's inclination toward history, especially in the past of Dorset, led to a natural attraction for old folktales, customs, and legends. These, handed down in the local dialect, often became the subjects of his poetry. His lifelong love of the outdoors, and his corresponding curiosity for natural phenomena, prompted him to examine closely his surroundings in the Vale of Blackmore and to use this as the setting for most of his work. The Dorset settings undoubtedly influenced the choice of writing in the Dorset dialect. Finally, his passion for philology and the study of language led to his analysis of the local dialect and to the discovery of its poetic possibilities. Like Hopkins after him, Barnes was quick to realize the value of older, less familiar words in literary diction. This tendency toward the fresh and original was, in large measure, responsible for Barnes's choice of language.

Poetic Techniques

While it was Barnes's intention to write "homely rhymes," those which praised the life and values of the simple, hard-working rural Englishman and those written in such language that the subjects of the poems could understand them, the poet used many sophisticated poetic devices in his verse. Many of these devices Barnes gleaned from his readings in the literatures of other cultures; some of the more arcane techniques he adopted for his own poetry are probably employed there for the first time in English. These devices are common in both Barnes's dialect verse and those poems written in "common English."

A good example of such a device is his poem "Green" which is an imitation of the Persian poetic form called a *ghazal,* a lyric varying in length from five to fifteen couplets, all with the same rhyme:

> Our summer way to church did wind about
> The cliff, where ivy on the *ledge* was *green* [my italics].
> Our summer way to town did skirt the wood,
> Where shining leaves, in tree and *hedge,* were *green.*[6]

Another device borrowed from the Persian involves the matching of sounds in half lines. An example of this occurs in Barnes's poem "The Wold Wall" when the persona exclaims, "Ah! well-a-day! O was adieu!" This punlike refrain unfortunately is repeated at the end of each stanza in the poem, providing proof once again that not all prosodic experimentation is successful.

Barnes borrowed from the Hebrew, as well. A device called "psalmic parallelism" is used in "Melhill Feast":

> Then by the orchards dim and cool,
> And then along Woodcombe's elmy side,
> And then by the meads, where waters glide,
> *Shallow by shallow, pool by pool* [my italics].
>
> And then to the house, that stands alone,
> With roses around the porch and wall,
> Where up by the bridge the waters fall,
> *Rock under rock, and stone by stone.*
>
> (P, 738)

As Geoffrey Grigson points out, Barnes also used another Eastern form called "adorning."[7] This device involves the matching of each word in a line with another in the next line. The matching may be in rhyme or metrical quantity as in "As trees be bright / Wi' bees in flight."

But the poet's interests were not confined to the Middle East. His involvement with linguistics and history led him to the study of medieval and older literature. Always experimenting, Barnes's work with old texts spilled over into his own poetry. In "The Lane," for example, he uses an alliterative formula reminiscent of Old English poetry:

> And where the ashes white bough whips
> The whistling air with coal-black tips;
> And where the grassy ground, beside
> The gravel-washing brook lies wide,
> And leaping lambs, with shrill-toned throats,
> Bleat loudly in their first white coats.
>
> (P, 664–65)

He borrows from the Irish, too, adopting the medieval device of "underrhyme," as in "Times of the Year":

> Soon shall grass, a-vrosted *bright* [my italics]
> Glishten *white* instead of green,
> An' the wind shall smite the *cows,*

Where the *boughs* be now their screen.
Things do change as years do vlee;
What ha' years in store vor me?

(*P, 415*)

Barnes has a special interest in Welsh, probably because the language survived so well, and because it was still a vital tongue and not just an object of curiosity. The old Celtic bards were an important area of his studies; it was from them that he took the convention of "cymmeriad," or resumption. This is the repetition of a word or thought at the beginning of a verse or stanza, analogous to the refrain, which repeats words at the end of the verse. Barnes adopted this device in poems such as "The Rest," calling it "verse-head."

The Dorset poet anticipates Hopkins in his use of another Welsh device, *cynghanedd,* which is a consonantal sound pattern set up in a line—or adjacent lines—of poetry. A good example of Barnes's use of this occurs in "My Orcha'd in Linden Lea." The line "Do leän down low in Linden Lea" establishes the sound pattern *L N D N L* in the first half of the line and repeats it in the second.

The Welsh art of *pennillion,* or what the medieval Scots poets called *flyting,* is reflected in Barnes's *running down.* Running down—a popular Dorset pastime, according to the poet—is basically deprecation of a person, object, or idea, as in "that contract is not worth the paper it's written on." The speaker is not, most often, being unfriendly, but is attempting to establish his or her good taste or judgment. An example in Barnes's poetry can be found in "Woak Wer Good Enough Woonce," in which the poet complains that while good English oak was once used as the basic building material, now people are not satisfied unless mahogany and other more exotic woods are used. He deprecates the new woods and the new habits and says that he will stick to his old standby, oak.

The willingness to experiment technically, to adapt conventions and techniques from other literatures to his own work was one of the main reasons that other poets were attracted to his verse. Patmore and Hopkins, both experimenters themselves, were among Barnes's most fervent admirers. And Thomas Hardy, a pioneer in both poetry and prose, learned much from Barnes's example.

Barnes's Language, Genres, and Subjects

Barnes's first book was *Poetical Pieces,* self-published in 1820 and consisting of ten poems written in what the poet came to call national English. Two years later, he brought out *Orra: A Lapland Tale,* a romantic narrative involving the search of a young girl for her lover. Both of these were printed in Dorchester and distributed locally. While he continued to write poetry, he did not bring out another volume of verse until 1844, when *Poems of Rural Life in the Dorset Dialect* was published. This achieved some degree of popularity, as new editions were brought out in 1847, 1862, and 1866. All of his work was not in the Dorset dialect, however, and his 1846 volume, *Poems Partly of Rural Life in National English,* was written in standard English. In 1859, Barnes published *Hwomely* [sic] *Rhymes: A Second Collection of Poems in the Dorset Dialect;* a second edition of this work was printed four years later. By 1862, he had added enough verses to bring out *Poems of Rural Life in the Dorset Dialect: Third Collection,* which was reprinted later in 1869, a year after his second collection of standard English poems, *Poems of Rural Life in Common English.* The 1844, 1859, and 1862 dialect collections were brought together in one volume, *Poems of Rural Life in the Dorset Dialect* (1879), and reissued several times afterward. Bernard Jones, who collected all the poetry in 1962, comments, "Such a record represents a solid poetic achievement, and to it should be added the American editions of *Hwomely Rhymes* in 1864 and of *Poems of Rural Life in Common English* in 1869" (*P,* 3).[8]

While he did continue to write and to publish poems in standard English after bringing out his dialect poems, Barnes is noted today almost exclusively for the latter. Indeed, during the nineteenth century, too, his fame rested on the poetry written in the rural tongue; the volumes which Coventry Patmore enthusiastically sent to Gerard Manley Hopkins in 1886 were the three editions of poems in the Dorset dialect.

In commenting on Barnes's use of the dialect, a choice which probably made his poetry difficult for the average reader and thus limited his potential for popularity, Thomas Hardy says that Barnes "couldn't help it."[9] The implication seems to be that since the Dorset dialect is the language the poet grew up with, it became the natural vehicle for his creative expression. Others, including Geoffrey Grigson[10] and Barnes's biographer-daughter,[11] disagree, citing the poet's philological studies as the main impetus for his choice. His linguistics studies led him to consider the Dorset speech as being more forceful and more poetic than the corrupted national English; as such, he saw it as appropriate to poetic expression, being a pure form of the language inherited from King Alfred and his forebears:

> Thus derived, the Dorset dialect is a broad and bold shape of the English language, as the Doric was of Greek. It is rich in humour, strong in raillery and hyperbole; and altogether as fit a vehicle of rustic feeling and thought, as the Doric is found in the *Idyllia* of Theocritus. Some people, who may have been taught to consider it as having originated from corruption of the written English, may not be prepared to hear that it is not only a separate offspring from the Anglo-Saxon tongue, but purer and more regular than the dialect which is chosen as the national speech; purer, inasmuch as it uses many words of Saxon origin, for which the English substitutes others of Latin, Greek, or French derivation; and more regular, inasmuch as it inflects regularly many words which, in the national language, are irregular. In English, purity is in many cases given up for the sake of what is considered to be elegance. [12]

It is clear that Barnes considered the use of Dorset not so much a break from tradition as a continuation of it. The poet seems more at ease with the dialect, too. Some of the common English poems— there are some notable exceptions—lack enthusiasm and even, at times, conviction. Other marked dissimilarities are apparent; for example, the dialect poems usually have an easily discernible dramatic structure. A persona can usually be identified, and he or she is usually speaking from a clearly marked setting, sometimes even from an actual geographic locality. An auditor is often present, as well; the resulting dramatic monologues do as much as the landscapes of John Constable to capture the life of country folk in nineteenth-century rural England. "Uncle Out O' Debt an' Out O' Danger" and "The Settle an' the Girt Wood Vire" use this dramatic technique. The majority of the common English poems, on the other hand, are presented from the point of view of the poet-persona, there is no identifiable audience, and in many instances the setting is not as readily apparent or vividly portrayed; "Season Tokens," and "The Parrock" are good examples. While many of the national English poems have been taken from earlier dialect versions, those

verses which are "translated" from Dorset to national English lose
something—perhaps authenticity.[13]

The dialect Barnes used when writing the dialect poems was that
spoken around Sturminster Newton in Dorset during the early nineteenth century. According to authorities, there is a distinct difference between the speeches of Sturminster and of Dorchester, the
latter, of course, being the one which Thomas Hardy used in his
work (cf. P, 17). Bernard Jones describes the language of Sturminster
as flowing and melodious, while that of Dorchester, he says, is more
staccato. Barnes imitates the Dorset speech of his particular locality
while at the same time applying the laws of language as he under-
stands them from his philological studies. The fact that some Dorset
expressions are revised from one edition to the next suggests that
Barnes changed some of his concepts concerning Dorset as time went
on (cf. P, 18).

Always the experimenter, the poet tried a number of genres for
his poetry. Since he was an admirer of Petrarch all his life, it was
natural for him to write Italian sonnets. We find several sonnets
among the early pieces, like "I Saw A Boy" and "Two Trees Were
We," and they are sprinkled among the later national English poems
as well. "In Ev'ry Dream Thy Lovely Features Rise" and "In Tender-
ness To Me Whom Thou Didst Spurn" are examples of later sonnets.
It is clear that Barnes shared Hopkins's feeling that this verse form
offered an opportunity for that perfect blend of structure and expression. Among the dialect poems, though, we find few sonnets, perhaps because Barnes felt they were inappropriate. Instead, he turns
to the eclogue, in many cases, in his attempts to re-create conver-
sations between the simple folk of Dorset. He presents monologues
in the dialect, too, sometimes in a dramatic setting with a clearly
identifiable auditor, other times as a rustic soliloquy in which the
speaker reflects and comments on his life or environment. He ex-
perimented early with the romance in *Orra: A Lapland Tale* and
later with the drama when he wrote *Ruth,* a short Bible play. He
composed hymns to be used in his services, as well as some verses
he calls "Sabbath Lays" which are short, Psalm-like poems which
extend the idea of an epigraph quoted from scripture. In his first
volume of poems written in national English, he follows Boccaccio
and Chaucer in offering a "tale of tales," in which several narrators
recount episodes in verse of a long story. Like Hopkins, Barnes
seems content to confine his experimentation to language—diction

and syntax especially—and to prosody; neither poet seems inclined
to attempt the invention of new forms.

In terms of content, Barnes's poems can all be assigned to one of
some six classes, each reflecting a subject of the poet's interest. The
subjects of the groups are autobiography and love, social issues and
politics, nature, religion, folktales and legends, and homely subjects. The last classification takes a name used by the poet himself
which is used to signify those verses that describe the rural life.
Naturally, there is some overlap; a love poem may have some homely
aspects, for example, or a religious poem may include some natural
description. But since the poems do seem to fall into one or another
of the categories, this system, an artificial one like any other, will
help discussion of the works.

Poems of Love and Bereavement

The first group—poems of autobiography and love—is comprised
of two topics which are inextricably welded together in Barnes's
poetry, love and bereavement. The man had one great love affair,
that one with his wife, Julia. He had met her when he was a young
man in Dorchester, she having moved there at age sixteen when her
father was transferred in his position of exciseman for the government. Barnes claimed that he fell in love with Julia Miles upon
first setting eyes upon her; he took great delight in later years in
telling his children that at their first meeting in 1818 he knew she
was to be his wife. By 1820, he had published in the *Weekly Entertainer* "To Julia," a poem which publicly declared his love for the
young lady. They did not immediately marry, however, because his
position as a lawyer's clerk did not provide him with enough salary
to support a wife. In 1823, a schoolmaster's position became vacant
at Mere, a town in the vicinity; Barnes applied and was accepted.
While the new position made it necessary to leave Dorchester and
Julia, Barnes took it on since it offered better pay and a chance in
the future for the young couple. After four years the waiting was
over; William and Julia were married and settled down in Mere in
1826. Their marriage was a happy and productive one, both of them
working hard to provide for their six children and to carry out the
duties of operating a school. This contented life went on until 1853
when Julia died after an illness, leaving William still a relatively
young man with children to raise. The death was a great shock, of

course, and Barnes never quite got over it. His journals, but most
of all his poems, remind us that he missed her a great deal.

His love poems reflect his love for his wife and later, his sense
of bereavement. Many of the verses seem to be autobiographical in
that so many female characters in or objects of his poems take on
qualities he attributes to Julia. In "The Maid Vor My Bride," for
instance, a young man enumerates the qualities of the girl he is in
love with. These qualities are ones which he admired in his wife
and, indeed, in all women. She is meek, kind, good, but not
scatterbrained. The girl, "is little lik' too many maïdens bezide,"
a real rarity, and she is "Not branten [brazen], nor spitevul, nor
wild; she've a mind / To think o' what's right, an' a heart to be
kind (P, 187). The paragon of probity and virtue, the lass nonetheless is physically attractive, with white skin, peachlike cheeks,
and a lithesome figure: 'She's pretty a-zitten; but oh! how my love /
Do watch her to madness when woonce [once] she do move" (P,
188). Many of the other love poems follow the pattern of the en-
amored rustic raising paeans to the object of his affection, Barnes's
obvious—and successful—attempt to adapt the pastoral eclogue to
a Dorsetshire setting. The attributes of a number of young women,
named variously Jennie, Jeanie, and Fanny, are praised in vivid
dialect verse by moonstruck young men. But the love poems contain
more than just representations of dairymaids, too; courtship is described, successful marriages are discussed, promises are made, and
betrothals are broken. Love and marriage are examined from the
point of view of both partners, and occasionally, Barnes uses a female
persona. Most often, though, the point of view is that of the male
lover, as in the dialect poem "In the Stillness o' Night."

Here, courtship, or at least the early stages of it, is described by
the young man who travels

> A-hoppen over geätes an' bars,
> By twinklen light o' winter stars,
> When snow do clumper to my shoe;
> An' zometimes we do slyly catch
> A chat an hour upon the stratch,
> An' peärt wi' whispers at the hatch
> In the stillness of the night.
>
> (P, 173)

The dialect makes the innocence even more poignant, it seems, just as it adds to the earnestness of the young beleaguered lover in "A Zong." Here, that age-old dilemma faced by young lovers—demands of the family in the choice of mate and the resultant loyalty crisis—is apparent. The problem is succinctly put:

> My kinsvo'k would faïn zee me teäke for my meäte
> A mäid that ha' wealth, but a maïd I should heäte;
> But I'd sooner leäbour wi' thee vor my bride,
> Than live lik' a squier wi' any beside.

Barnes's persona rejects the cold logic of Tennyson's new style northern farmer, and demonstrates his old-fashioned reluctance to break a promise:

> My head's in the storm, but my root's in the rock.
> Zoo, Jenny, don't sobby! vor I shall be true;
> Noo might under heaven shall peärt me vrom you.
>
> (P, 187)

Love like this, Barnes knew, does not fade with marriage although it might change directions; the mature relationship is often strengthened by adversity. In "Jeane," the husband, after recounting the blissful courtship, tells of the evolution of a ten year marriage:

> An' nwone but I can ever tell
> Ov all thy tear that have a-vell
> When trials meäde thy boson swell,
>   An' nwone but thou o' mine, Jeäne;
> An' now my heart, that heav'd wi' pride
> Back then to have thee at my zide, Do love thee mwore
> as years do slide,
>   An' leave them times behine, Jeäne.
>
> (P, 214)

As an observer of the human scene, though, the poet knew that lovers do not always live happily ever after. In "Meary Wedded," Barnes tries to depict the desolation left behind when a young swain's loved one goes off to marry another. The pathetic fallacy, mainstay metaphor of the adolescent heart, is much in evidence as the young man views his world. He echoes Mariana in the moated grange as he looks around the seemingly empty farmstead saying, "Our's is now a lifeless pleace." Even the animals are affected:

> The dog that woonce wer glad to bear
> Her fondlen vingers down his hëair,
> Do leän his head ageän the vloor,
> To watch, wi' heavy eyes, the door . . .
> (P, 216)

Barnes's use of dialect and rhyme contribute to the overall bathetic effect of this portrait of the self-indulgent teenager. He treats more seriously, though, the plight of a young girl deserted by her lover. While it is not explicitly stated, perhaps Barnes is sympathizing with the vulnerability of an unmarried woman in a small conservative community who has succumbed to the charms of an unfaithful man. Jane of Buckley-hill is one such maiden who is deserted so that the man is free to marry a woman "with gold":

> For she had walk'd with him, poor maid,
> Word-trusting down to the grove's dim shade,
> And lov'd him, since she thought him true.
> (P, 648)

Many of Barnes's love poems are a direct reflection of the loss of his wife, Julia. "Plorata Veris Lachrymis" is a good example. The speaker, clearly the poet, says that life has lost "its hope and zest" since the bride's death, and that sights which brought pleasure when they were together now bring only pain. He concludes this painful, sincere, but conventional poem by remarking that he does not care about his own life's waning if this means that their souls will meet again. "My Dearest Julia" continues in this sentimental but doubtless therapeutic vein. Here the persona, again clearly the poet, admits that sometimes he is distracted from his loss:

> where joyful faces crowd
> And merry tongues are ringing loud,
> Or where some needful work unwrought
> May call for all my care and thought,
> Or where some landscape, bath'd in light,
> May spread to fascinate my sight,
> Thy form may melt awhile, as fade

> Our shades within some welkin shade.
>
> <div align="right">(<i>P</i>, 703)</div>

But when he realizes this distraction, the persona says that he feels chastened, that he seems to hear Julia's voice admonishing him for forgetting his loss, even momentarily, in the light of all her years of work and care during their marriage. If this is not a pose—and Barnes is not a poseur—then the supposed admonishment displays an attitude toward his bereavement which is so scrupulous that it borders on the morbid. Guilt is obvious here, while the basis for guilt is obscure. In none of the biographical material—although the major source of the details of his life is Lucy Baxter, a daughter and scarcely an objective critic—is there any hint of enmity or even tension between William and Julia. While psychological analysis is clearly outside the province of this work, it should be noted here that Barnes's mother, like Julia an intelligent, strong, and capable person, died when he was very young, too young, perhaps, for him to frame his sorrow in appropriate conventional devices such as elegiac poems. The almost overscrupulousness of the mourning for the wife could be explained by a nagging feeling of inadequateness about the mourning for the mother. This speculation is fueled by another poem, "The Morning Moon."

In this poem, the persona—the poet—relates the story of an early morning walk which takes him to the house, now deserted, where his mother had lived. The house reminds him of his mother and what she had meant to him:

> And she, dear soul, so good and kind,
> Had holden long, in my young mind,
> Of holy thought, the highest place
> Of honour, for her love and grace.

But then some new thoughts enter in:

> But now my wife to heart and sight
> May seem to shine a fuller light;
> And as the sun may rise to view,
> To dim the moon from pale to blue,
>   My comely bride
>   May seem to hide
> My mother, now my morning moon.

(P, 771–72)

The traveler then vows never to let his affection for his wife obscure the memory of his dead mother. The poem is interesting in that it indicates a link, perhaps a tension, existing between the feelings for his mother and those for his wife. This link was no doubt strengthened after Julia's death when Barnes once again was left alone.

His sense of loss doubtlessly contributed to the beauty of some of his best poetry. "The Leady's Tower," written shortly after Julia's death, is a look at his own grief seen through the eyes of a fellow Dorsetman. The persona describes a walking tour taken with a local clergyman. The clergyman, a Mr. Collins, is a character in many of Barnes's dialect narratives, depicted as a gentle, intelligent commentator upon country scenes and events. He serves as an advisor to the Dorset folk; doubtless Barnes considered him to be a model of the rural preacher or schoolmaster.

In this poem, the narrator and Mr. Collins have come to the top of a hill where they find a tower, apparently not noticed previously by the speaker, as he asks the preacher, " 'What is it then theäse tower do meän / A-built so feäir, an' kept so cleän?' " The good parson answers that it is grief that has caused the building to be erected. He goes on to say that the owner, a squire, has all the earthly accoutrements anyone could want; he is not happy, though, because "His woone true friend, his wife, is dead." The squire has erected the tower to show his grief. Mr. Collins explains it like this:

> Zoo now her happy soul's a-gone,
> An' he in grief's a-ling'ren on,
> Do do his heart zome good to show
> His love to flesh and blood below.
> An' zoo he rear'd, wi' smitten soul,
> Theäse Leädy's Tower upon the knowl.
>
> (P, 253)

"The Leady's Tower" takes grief for a loved one as its subject, as does "My Darling Julia," but there are striking differences in the two poems. "The Leady's Tower" is written in the Dorset dialect and narrated by a persona who is clearly sympathetic yet not involved directly in the squire's grief. "My Darling Julia" is much more personal in that the persona is the grieved one, yet the grief is as intense in the poem in which it is demonstrated as it is in the one in which it is stated.

Nowhere is Barnes's love for his wife and his grief for her loss shown more poignantly than in the companion pieces, "Wife A-Prais'd" and "The Wife A-Lost," both written in dialect. The first, as the title suggests, praises the wife not only for her comeliness, but also for her good humor, her grace, and "busy hands a-tweilen [toiling] on." The persona speaks of his attraction for the young woman who seems to effuse a Wordsworthian harmony with the natural surroundings:

> An' there, wi' heäir o' glossy black,
> Bezide your neck an' down your back,
> You rambled gaÿ a-bloomen feäir,
> By boughs o' maÿ a-bloomen feäir;
> An' while the birds did twitter nigh,
> An' water weäves did glitter nigh,
> You gather'd cowslips in the lew,
> Below the vallèn dew.
>
> (P, 332)

The attraction that the persona feels for the girl does not dissipate with age; after they are married, the woman's mature attributes come into bloom:

> An' now, while you've a-been my bride
> As years o' flow'rs bloom'd an' died,
> Your smilen feäce ha' been my jöy;
> Your soul o' greäce ha' been my jöy;
> An' wi' my evenen rest a-come,
> An' zunsheen to the west a-come
> I'm glad to teäke my road to you
> Vrom vields of vallen dew.
>
> (P, 333)

But in the companion piece, "The Wife A-Lost," Barnes describes the reluctance of the bereaved husband to stay in the house that the couple shared, indeed, his reluctance to visit places where they had been together. Now, the persona says, he would rather be in a place "Where you did never come" (*P, 334*).

Social and Political Poems

E. M. Forster, in his essay on Barnes in *Two Cheers for Democracy,* makes the statement that Barnes's amiability prevented him from dealing with the social issues of the day. "He could live through the Labourers' Revolt of 1830 without its shadows falling across his verse," Forster says, with the same innocence with which he helps his neighbor Colonel Shrapnel with some mathematical formulae for his new explosive shell.[14] In the forewords to his edition of Barnes's poems, Bernard Jones rightly takes issue with Forster. Jones says,

It never seemed likely that a man like Barnes should be unaware of such things. . . . The social agitation of 1830, indeed, turned his mind to the working classes of land folk around him and led him to write a series of eclogues of the greatest importance to the social historian and to anyone who would understand the making of William Barnes the poet. (*P, 12*)

Indeed, just as Forster errs in asserting that Barnes helped Shrapnel develop the explosive shell which bears his name, he is mistaken in his statement about Barnes's political innocence. In the series of eclogues Jones is referring to, the poet addresses the major issues confronting the English rural poor in the first half of the nineteenth century: enclosure, emigration, the poor laws and workhouses, the value and dignity of labor, land allotments, machine-induced unemployment, and the organization of the working man.

Barnes's concern for the unlanded poor is demonstrated in his dialect eclogue, "The 'Lotments," a poem depicting a conversation between two Dorsetmen, John and Richard. John, who lives in another neighborhood, had come upon Richard working his small patch of earth, and wonders if all the activity is worth the trouble:

> D'ye think 'tis beter wi' it than without it?
> A'reck'nen rent, an' time, an' zeed to stock it,
> D'ye think that you be anything in pocket?
>   (*P, 94*)

The laborer assures his friend that the toil is profitable for a number of reasons. First of all, he says, it gives him the opportunity

to work at useful employment, an end in itself. Second, he is able
to bring up his children properly, and his friend John agrees:

> Vor woone [one] must know a deäl about the land
> Bevore woone's fit to lend a useful hand,
> In geärden or a-vield upon a farm.

(P, 94)

In addition to the education it provides, Richard goes on, tending
the little plot keeps the children out of mischief:

> An' then the work do keep them out o' harm;
> Vor vo'ks that don't do nothen will be vound
> Soon doen woorse than nothen, I'll be bound.

(P, 94)

And naturally, there are the economic rewards that access to a
piece of land, albeit a small one, is able to bring to the hard-working
family. Richard enumerates some of these when he says,

> wi' theäse here bit
> O' land, why I have ev'ry thing a' mwost [almost]:
> Vor I can fatten vowels [fowls] vor the spit,
> Or zell a good fat goose or two to rwoast . . .

(P, 95.)

By the end of the conversation, John is impressed and envious,
saying that with a little piece of ground he would be able to keep
himself "from parish," meaning that he could keep his family from
going on the welfare rolls.

The eclogue shows Barnes's belief in the dignity of labor, however
common, a stance that he takes often in his verse and also in his
economic treatise, *Views of Labour and Gold*. Both characters yearn
for the opportunity for honest work, but it is only Richard who is
allowed it because of the generosity of his squire. After enclosure,
the plight of the poor people in rural England became acute. During
the Napoleonic Wars, their situation was especially bad; to allow
them some relief, the practice of renting parcels of the large estates
to those willing to work the ground was introduced. Richard's
" 'lotment" is one such parcel, but as the poem indicates, this system
was not prevalent enough to give widespread relief. While Richard's

squire has seen fit to lease some of his land, this is not true in John's area:

> I wish the girt woones [great ones] had a-got the greäce
> To let out land lik' this in over pleäce;
> But I do fear there'll never be nwone vor us,
> An' I can't tell whatever we shall do:
> We be a'most a-starven, an' we'd goo
> To 'merica, if we'd enough to car us [carry us, pay our fare].
>
> (P, 94)

It is clear that the rural poor were at the mercy of the "girt woones" who maintained property and managed the wealth of the country. William Cobbett and others spoke out against the growing strength of the wealthy agricultural class who controlled the agricultural system of England. These landed gentry Cobbett saw as being irresponsible, interested only in making a profit, and as differing greatly from the former resident native gentry, who were interested in the land and those who tilled it. The poor laws, designed to help the unlanded working class, actually worked to their detriment. Especially odious was the "Speenhamland system" which paid poor relief to supplement the wages of the working poor. In the short run, the system benefited the poor, but in the long term it exacerbated the problem in that it relieved the employer of the responsibility of paying a living wage. In addition, it forced the parish ratepayer or taxpayer to pay part of the wage expense of the big farmer or factory owner.

An alternative to those farm laborers with the boat fare was emigration to the United States, Canada, or Australia. Barnes deals with this phenomenon in his eclogue "Rusticus Emigrans Emigration" which depicts a conversation between Robert and his friend Richard who is about to emigrate. Richard talks first about the physical facts of the trip, a natural beginning for two practical men of the soil. He tells about the plans to leave for London on the next Sunday, following the family belongings he had packed up in a barrel and sent on ahead. Answering his friend's queries, Richard goes on to decribe how the women and children will ride in a wagon while the men walk alongside. The voyage itself, he goes on to say, will last fourteen weeks, with the passengers subject to crowding and seasickness.

Then Robert asks about the spiritual aspects of the venture, how the other feels about leaving the land of his birth. Richard admits that it is difficult to go:

> Here be the ground where I've worked and played;
> Here is the hut that I wer barn and bred in;
> Here is the little church where we've a prayed,
> And churchyard that my kinsvolk's buones be laid in;
> And I myzelf, you know, should like to lie
> Among 'em too when I do come to die.
>
> (*P*, 483–84)

But Richard realizes that he has no choice but to leave England; Robert agrees, as he knows the economic realities well enough:

> 'Tis hard a man can't get a luöaf to veed 'en [feed them]
> Upon the pliäce wher life wer vust a gied 'en [first given to them];
> 'Tis hard that if he'd work, there's noo work, var'n [for him],
> Or that his work woon't bring enough o' money
> To keep 'en, though the land is vull of carn [full of corn]
> And cattle; and do flow wi' milk and honey.
>
> (*P*, 484)

Robert's ironic contrasting of the condition of England's agriculture with the condition of her poor is not lost on Richard, who blames the economic system and the greed of those who control it:

> They that 'ave got the wordle's [world's] goods, no doubt on't,
> Do like it, and ben't [aren't] willing to go out on't;
> There's nothin her var I [for me] but want and zorrow,
> Zoo I don't mind o' leaven it to-morrow.
> If 'twerden var [it weren't for] my children and my wife,
> I wou'dent gi' a zixpence var my life.
>
> (*P*, 484–85)

The poem ends with Robert bidding his friend farewell with a two-line admonition to put his faith in God. In spite of this call for trust in God, the rhetorical thrust of the poem is clearly bitter, and Barnes is directly critical of the economic system which forces the English yeomanry into bankruptcy and, for all practical purposes, deportation. Not only could he see the individual suffering

surrounding emigration, but he felt that the result of such a policy
was the depletion of England's root-stock, the destruction of the
descendants of farmers who stood with Alfred and all the other kings
down through England's tumultuous history.

In 1834 the whole system of poor laws was revised, after a commission investigated the situation and issued its report, resulting
in the Poor Law Amendment Act. The commission addressed itself
mainly to the able-bodied poor, those able and willng to work and
those able but less willing. The amendment led to the establishment
of a series of workhouses, in which the aged, orphan children, the
insane, and the able-bodied poor were ostensibly to be treated separately, but the theory was not always carried out in practice. Often,
all of the indigent were herded together and treated indiscriminately.
The officials in charge were often petty despots who terrorized their
charges. Charles Dickens depicted life in the poorhouse and those
who made it unbearable in *Oliver Twist* and other novels, goading
the consciences of many smug Victorians, and other writers and
commentators followed suit. Barnes was one of these social critics;
he examines the new system and finds it wanting in his eclogue
"Rusticus Res Politicas Animadvertens: The New Poor Laws." Here
again two Dorsetman, John and Thomas, discuss the new and old
laws concerning the poor. By way of introduction they both agree
that poor relief is best avoided. As Thomas says,

> I hope to kip myzelf till I da die,
> An' miäke my own han's always veed my jaes [feed my jaws]
> I alëways scarn'd as I da hope to scarn
> To ax vor [ask for] money that I diden yeärn [earn].
>
> (*P*, 487)

Yet both know that poor relief for some, given the contemporary
economic climate, is inevitable. The men register shock and dismay
when they recount how men are treated when they apply for help:

> Zoo if a man should come to want relief,
> An' goo an' ax the auverzeer var't [overseer of it],
> Tha'l tiäke an' put en up into a cart,
> An' car en [carry him] out o' parish like a thief,
> An' shove en in to bed an' tiäble,
> Amang a house vull o' fresh fiäzes [faces],
> Wi' scores o' volk vrom fifty pliäzes

> Like hosses in a common stiäble.
>
> > (*P, 488*)

Once the family is admitted to the workhouse, the degradation continues. The able-bodied poor and the unemployed are thrown together with the aged and the insane. Because of the crowded conditions, there is a lack of privacy for individuals, let alone couples, and the family unit and marital relationships are subjected to tremendous stress. John's comments on the problems of couples in the poorhouse, although made with wry and sardonic humor, reflect the pathos of the situation:

> Aye, they be quain [are going to] ya know, to kip asunder [keep apart]
> The menvolk in the poorhouse, vrom their wives.
> How wull the women like thick [this] plan I wonder?
> They mid [might] as well, I think, each wi' his bride
> Go back to church an' have ther knot untied.
>
> > (*P, 488*)

The social theory behind the workhouses is discussed by the two Dorsetmen in the second half of the poem. Thomas rather self-righteously points out that perhaps the institutions, known as "Bastilles" by the poor, serve as inspirations to the poor. This is much like the theory prevalent in many quarters today which espouses the use of the electric chair as an educational tool. Thomas says,

> Ees, that's an oddish job; but mid [might] be good,
> Var they da want to bring volk, if they can,
> To have muore forezight; and' to miäke a man
> Trust only to his zelf var food.
>
> > (*P, 488*)

But he then goes on to describe his own life, how he has always worked hard, and how he has been granted his very freedom because of his labor.

> An' veel that I be free, an' tell my name
> To al the wordle [world] without fear or shiäme.
> But if I wer a liäzy man, an' willen
> To zell my freedom for a parish shillen,
> I must a skulked about a looken down

Wi' shiäme and' mieänness, like a slinken houn'.

(P, 489)

This belief in the worth and the power of work expressed by the words of a Dorset farmer is precisely what some other Victorian writers and social critics were saying at the time. An example can be found in Thomas Carlyle's *Past and Present:*

Consider how, even in the meanest sorts of labour, the whole soul of a man is composed into a kind of real harmony, the instant he sets himself to work! Doubt, Desire, Sorrow, Remorse, Indignation, Despair itself, all these like helldogs lie beleaguering the soul of the poor dayworker, as of every man: but he bends himself with free valour against his task, and all these are stilled, all these shrink murmuring far off into their caves. The man is now a man. [15]

Farmer Thomas agrees with this idea even if his mode of expressing it differs from Carlyle's. Diligence and honesty to him are virtues; he has taught his children to "yarn ther bread, an' shun a crime."

John agrees, and the poem ends as he elaborates on the principle and develops this idea. He says that if society wishes to make the poor industrious and moral people, it should value industry and morality in its citizens rather than riches and vanity. The ideas expressed here by the yeoman farmer follow closely those expressed by Barnes in *Views of Labour and Gold* concerning the intrinsic worth of the individual and the essential dignity of labor. John says,

But then if volk da want to miäke the poor
Good men they ought to value fiävour goodness muore.
Volk do esteem a rogue in a high pliäce
Muore than a poorer man that's rich in griäce.

(P, 489)

The world, he says, places more value on appearances—on clothes, Carlyle would say—than on the realities of virtue.

His final comment on the laws and society's attitudes toward the poor is couched in an appropriate agricultural metaphor:

Thiëse laes mid [these laws might] do some good; but volk mast show
Esteem var goodness if they'd zee it grow.

A farmer woulden git much vrom his zeeds
If they were left to struggle wi' the weeds.

(P, 489)

The enclosure acts of the eighteenth and early nineteenth centuries had always hurt the poor, but by the 1820s and 1830s, the problem had become acute. Until enclosure, most of the fields were open and some were held in common by all of the members of a locality. This meant in practice that a cottager, who most likely owned only the land his home stood on plus a small garden plot for raising vegetables, was able to keep a few domestic animals. Poultry, hogs, and even cows were able to acquire a great deal of their sustenance by feeding on the common ground. Even the waste lands—the moors—were important to the cottagers because the small brush which grew there along with animal dung collected from the fields often offered the only source of fuel for the poor. The furze cutters in Thomas Hardy's novels are good examples of people using the waste land for fuel. After enclosure, though, these sources of support for the cottager were removed when control of the fields went over to the large farmers. The fields, open for centuries, were closed to all but their owners, and even many of the waste lands were denied to the poor because improved agricultural methods made them valuable as farm land. The small landowners, not able to survive with only their small garden plots to sustain them, had to choose between becoming agricultural laborers or factory hands, both menial and low-paid occupations. As we have seen, the only other doors open to them were the gates of the poorhouse or the hatches of the emigration ships.

Barnes discusses this problem in another of his eclogues "The Common A-took In" using Thomas and John again as his personae. The two meet as John is on his way to sell his flock of geese at the market. Thomas asks why, "B'ye run aground?" John replies that he is in economic difficulty, that he must sell his poultry, and that he soon will be forced to sell his cow. "They do meän to teäke the moor in, I do hear," he says, and as a result his animals "woon't have any groun' to run on." He is able to relate the seriousness of the problem by describing the ancient system of farming used by the poor with its heavy reliance on the common ground:

Now I do mow

My bit o' grass, an' meäke a little rick;
An' in the zummer, while do grow,
My cow do run in common vor to pick
A bleäde or two o'grass, if she can vind em. . . .

His geese, too, run on the common ground, thus providing the
family with feathers to sell in the summer and goose meat in the
winter. They are dependent on the open land for other needs as
well:

Why I can teäke my hook an' gloves, an' goo
To cut a lot o' vuzz and briars
Vor heten ovens, or for lighten viers [fires].
An' when the children be too young to eärn
A penny, they can g'out in zunny weather,
An' run about, an' get together
A bag o' cow-dung vor to burn.

(P, 159)

With the dependency of the poor on the common established,
the poem ends on a note of uncertainty. Thomas hopes that the
rumors he has heard are true, and that the poor will be assigned
bits of ground (allotments) to supplement their own meager plots.
John replies that he hopes so too, for unless something is done, he
and his family have no recourse but the workhouse.

In the face of such desperate economic problems, it is no wonder
that movements arose which sought to unite the workers in cooperative efforts to relieve their plight. These efforts were hampered
somewhat by the existence of the Combination Laws, statutes passed
during the French wars around the turn of the century which made
trade unions illegal. By 1842, through the efforts of Francis Place,
Joseph Hume, and others, these acts were repealed, demonstrating
a certain amount of public sympathy for improvement of the worker's
condition. The next decade showed a substantial growth in the
formation of trade unions.

One of the most ambitious organizing ventures was called the
Grand National Consolidated Trades Union which at its height
numbered five hundred thousand laborers on its rolls. This union
was begun by Robert Owen, a middle-class idealist with utopian
plans. His first attempt at demonstrating his ideas on labor reform
was the experiment at New Lanark in 1800. Here he set up in the

mills a system of public health, education, and economic security for the workers. "The death-blow" to this organization, David Thomson reports, "was delivered by the government and judiciary in the shape of the famous Tolpuddle prosecution."[16]

The Tolpuddle prosecution came about after some agricultural workers from Dorset in 1834 organized a union which was to be affiliated with the Grand National Consolidated. According to testimony, some "reading" took place at an initiation for new members which "seemed to be out of some part of the Bible." Because of this, the men were tried and convicted of administering unlawful oaths, then sentenced to seven years transportation, or the equivalent of banishment. While the sentences were remanded two years later, the case, along with a number of unsuccessful strikes and lock-outs, brought about the demise of the union.[17]

Similar fates were suffered by similar organizations for similar reasons. The Chartist movement grew out of the same political and economic situation that spawned other protests. Elements of Owens's Grand National Consolidated Union joined with other trade unionists, with London artisans, and with workers in industrialized areas to form a major labor reform movement. Under the leadership of Francis Place, known as the radical tailor, and William Lovett, founder of the London Working Men's Association, the Chartists grew into a vital force in the political, economic, and social affairs of mid-nineteenth-century England. Lovett's and Place's Charter, drawn up in 1838, was based on six points: universal male suffrage; equal electoral districts; removal of the property qualifications for members of Parliament; payment for members of Parliament; secret ballot; and annual general elections.[18] While none of these seems very radical today, they were explosive issues in the 1830s and 1840s in Britain.

Of course, it is unlikely on the face of it that a man as close to the poor agricultural classes as Barnes was would be able to ignore events with national implications such as Tolpuddle, especially since the incident took place in his own neighborhood. Indeed, Jones reports in his notes to the collected edition of the poems that Barnes specified that his eclogue "The Times" was written with the Chartists in mind.

This poem, at first entitled "The Unioners," involves a discussion between two Dorset workingmen, one disposed toward the efforts at organizing workers, the other suspicious of the organizers. John

opens the conversation by asking Tom whether or not it is true that
he has joined the leaguers. Tom replies that low wages and high
prices have forced him to join. John is not so sure that organizing
is the answer. He says, "if they could meäke a shillen goo / In
market just so vur as two . . . I'd be their man."

Tom answers this rather unrealistic statment by outlining the
Chartist's political policy. First, he says, they would send up members to Parliament every year, elected by polls at which every man
would be able to vote. (Female suffrage was an issue too radical at
this time, apparently, even for the Chartists.) These members of
Parliament, Tom says, could even be from the working class, and
why not?

> Why shoulden fellows meäke good laws an' speeches
> A-dressed in fusti'n cwoats an' cord'roy breeches?
> Or why should hooks an' shovels, zives [scythes] an' oxes,
> Keep any man vrom voten o' the taxes?
> An' when the poor've a-got a sheäre
> In meäken laws, they'll teäke good ceäre
> To meäken zome good woones vor the poor.
>
> (P, 227)

John, however, does not trust any politicians—even working-
class ones—and he certainly is not about to put his fate in the hands
of strangers like the union organizers. He displays a xenophobic
rustic reticence to accept the fact that the union men are not out
to line their own pockets.

> An' as vor me, I don't know what to think
> O' them there fine, big talken, cunnen,
> Strange men, a-comen down vrom Lon'on.
> Why they don't stint their zelves, but eat an' drink
> The best at public-house where they do staÿ;
> They don't work gratis, they do get their paÿ.
> They woulden pinch their zelves to do us good,
> Nor gi'e their money vor to buy us food.
> D'ye think, if we should meet em in the street
> Zome day in Lon'on, they would stand a treat?
>
> (P, 229)

By way of illustration John goes on to relate a fable concerning a
pig and a crow. The crow, runs the fable, is hungry for some seeds

which farmers have just sown, but is unable to retrieve any. He proposes, "lik' a man at hustens," that the pig help him dig up the seed and that they share the grain. The pig agrees, roots in the ground, and turns up the kernels of barley which have recently been planted. The crow then picks up the grains with his bill, while the pig, with his much larger mouth, is not able to share in the feast. The farmer then arrives on the scene and proceeds to beat the pig while the crow flies off.

The implications of the allegory are not lost on Tom, but he is not convinced, as John is, of the organizers' evil motives. The poem ends indecisively, with neither man being won over to the other side. In all likelihood, the dilemma represents Barnes's feelings on the matter: while he saw the reasons behind and even the need for the organization of the laboring man, he was conservative and in-dependent enough to think that ultimately the problem would be solved by a coalition of the workers and the landed aristocracy. He seems sympathetic with the allotment system, for example, in which the enlightened landowner through his own choice turns over a portion of land to the energetic laborer to use as if he owned it. Barnes's sympathies were obviously with the poor and obviously pro-reform, but he saw change best coming about through a system like Disraeli's Radical Tory position, rather than through organized labor. The Radical Tory program was to introduce orderly change in those areas where reform was needed, while preserving the best of the traditions and institutions of the past.

The general plight of the rural poor is discussed in "Two Farmes in Woone [one]," an eclogue in which two characters, Robert and Thomas, converse about the consolidation of farm land and other problems. Thomas's employer is about to lose his farm to Farmer Tup, described as a "sly wold fellow" and a "Poor over-reachen man." Robert asks, "He don't want all the farms in parish, do er?" and Thomas is specific in his reply.

Why ees [yes], all he ever can come across.
Last year, you know, he got away the eäcre
Or two o' ground a-rented by the beäker,
An' what the butcher had to keep his hoss;
An' vo'k do beä'nhan' [people are of the opinion] now, that meäster's lot
Will be a-drow'd [thrown] along wi' what he got.

                                                        (*P*, 161),

The impact of such action on the community is discussed by the pair as well. Forced from their farms, many small farmers became day laborers working the fields of the large landowners like Farmer Tup. Their ability to support their families was thus greatly diminished. Fewer farmsteads meant fewer opportunities for masons, blacksmiths, carpenters, and other craftsmen, so these industries suffered, too. Perhaps the biggest impact, though, was the spiritual one: while all work is sacred to Barnes, working to improve one's own place is more sacred than working for wages. Land consolidation meant fewer opportunities for those inclined to a lifetime of farming, even for the most ambitious, as Robert explains:

> Aye, if a young chap, woonce, had any wit
> To try an' screäpe together zome vew pound,
> To buy zome cows and' teäke a bit o' ground,
> He mid [might] become a farmer, bit by bit.
>   (P, 161)

The farms now, though, he complains, are so big and the investment needed so expensive that a young man without ample means cannot even entertain the notion of owning his own place. By this time, too, there were few opportunities even to work as a day laborer or as a farmhand because of the influx of farm machinery. Efficient mowers, horse-drawn rakes, and threshing machines replaced men in the fields. The impact of farm machinery on the labor force was swift, it was implemented with little regard for the displaced workers, and it was profoundly resented, as Thomas makes clear:

> Why here wer vourteen men, zome years agoo,
> A-kept a-drashen [threshing] half the winter drough;
> An' now, woon's drashels [flails, threshing tools] be'n't a bit o' good.
> They got machines to drash [thresh] wi', plague teäke em!
> An' he that vust [first] vound out the way to meäke em,
> I'd drash his busy zides vorn [for him] if I could.
> Avore they took away our work, they ought
> To meäke us up our bread our leäbour bought.
>   (P, 162)

Far from ignoring the plight of the rural poor as Forster suggests, Barnes tried to act as their spokesman by depicting their economic and political dilemmas in a series of eclogues. These poems sought to portray the working man realistically in a believable setting, discussing his problems in his own language. Barnes uses as the subjects for these verses the major issues confronting the British rural poor in the first half of the nineteenth century, namely enclosure, emigration, land allotments, machine-induced unemployment, poor laws and workhouses, organization of the labor force, and the value and dignity of labor.

Nature Poems

In his treatise on aesthetics, "Thoughts on Beauty and Art," Barnes defines the beautiful in this way: "the beautiful in nature is the unmarred result of God's first creative or forming will, and that the beautiful in art is the result of an unmistaken working of man in accordance with the beautiful in nature."[19] Beauty in nature is to be celebrated, admired, and depicted in art because it serves as a clue to, or a hint at, or a fleeting glimpse of, the grandeur of God. Barnes says that although we do not find all of God's works in "the full beauty of His first-forming will"—many of these have been marred through various means—"there is yet so much of the beauty of God's primary work, that our minds can well rise from their marred shapes to the higher ones, or the beau ideal of which they may be spoilt forms; and that beau ideal is, in our opinion, one of the true objects of high art."[20] God's grandeur can be discovered in nature, and art can help in that discovery; the role of the artist is to aid the process, to use his insights and creativity, to lend his mind out like Browning's Fra Lippo Lippi.

Much of "Thoughts on Beauty and Art" is devoted to the beauty of form and proportion, especially that of natural and man-made curves, and the beauty of color, especially that of the juxtaposition of hues. These come together in landscapes, he says: "In the forms and colours of objects in a landscape there is a fitness and harmony of the good of God's formative will."[21] And it is not only unmarred nature that Barnes sees as beautiful, for "much of the beauty of a landscape arises from the harmony of its forms and hues, and the fitness of nature's yielders of good to their offices and the wants of man."[22] This fitness Barnes speaks of might be defined as an appropriateness which follows God's design. Examples might be the fitness of elasticity to a poplar so that is might bend in the wind instead of break; the fitness of sleekness to a cow so that it might yield more milk and meat to its owner; the fitness of the cool colors of grass and leaves so that they might absorb the heat of the sun. Objects in a landscape which suggest fitness are tokens of the presence of God while the landscape taken together implies "the harmony of the whole with the good of man."

Since a discussion of landscapes provides the focus of his treatise on aesthetics, it is little wonder that a great deal of his poetry consists of verbal depictions of landscapes. What John Constable did with oils and canvas, Barnes tried to do with pen and ink. Most of the nature poems rely heavily on description, as in "I Got Two Vields," in which the speaker says he would not trade his farm for any squire's estate. The farm is

> Where yollow clotes [water lilies], in spreaden beds
> O' floaten leaves, do lift their heads
> By benden bulrushes an' zedge
> A-swaÿen at the water's edge,
> Below the withy [willow] that do spread
> Athirt the brook his grey-leav'd head.
> An' eltrot flowers, milky white,
> Do catch the slanten evenen light;
> An' in the meäple boughs, along
> The hedge do ring the blackbird's zong;
> Or in the day, a-vlee-en drough [fleeing through]
> The leafy trees, the whoa'se gookoo [hoarse cuckoo]
> Do zing to mowers that do zet
> Their zives on end, an' stan' to whet.
> From my wold house among the trees
> A leäne do goo along the leäze [pasture]
> O' yollow gravel, down between
> Two mossy banks vor ever green. . . .
>
> (P, 126)

The description goes on in the poem creating an accumulation of detail which conjures the readers' minds visions of scenes like Constable's *The Cornfield,* or his landscapes of Dedham Vale and Hempstead, lush with vegetation, rich in color and detail.[23] Many of the nature poems are descriptions of landscapes of this sort, many, indeed, being word portraits of particular places. Just as the painter will depict a scene familiar to his audience, so does Barnes treat several particular neighborhoods in Dorset, as "Whitburn's Green and White," "Pentridge," and "The River Stour."

Like Hopkins, Barnes writes a number of nature sonnets in which a description of a scene or object in nature is given in the octave followed by an abstract commentary in the sestet on what the scene or object brings to the mind of the speaker-viewer. One example is "Evening Dreams." After a pleasant evening in a leafy arbor, the speaker says,

> Then how I lose myself in nameless dreams
> Of days long passed away, or yet to come;
> And things beyond the ken of worldly sight;
> Till ev'ry moving shade before me seems
> Some wand'ring spirit, bodiless and dumb,
> That glides along the shady earth at night.
>
> (P, 646)

In "Rural Nature," after a description of a country scene, the persona says,

> Give me the noisy town and let the great
> Ride might o'er the earth with pride and pow'r;
> Give avarice his gold: but let me flee
> Where cold and selfish hearts live not to hate
> And scorn. Oh, take me to thy lonely bow'r,
> Sweet rural nature! Life is dear for thee.
>
> (P, 637)

Years of teaching science by taking his students on field trips of the countryside certainly left Barnes with indelible impressions of much of the flora and fauna native to Dorset. In several of the nature poems these impressions are given voice. Each species is first described and then used as a controlling metaphor for a human mood, emotion, or condition. Often, too, particular natural phenomena act as catalysts to the memory of the speaker, bringing up incidents or situations from the past, much as the landscape a few miles above Tintern Abbey produced sensations from the past in the mind of William Wordsworth.

The down of a thistle is used as a controlling metaphor in "Thissledown," a didactic little verse which compares the bit of fluff tossed about by the wind to a person with no direction and with

no productive duty to perform. The down-puff, or what it stands
for, is to be pitied, the speaker says, because it has lost its reason
for being:

> Zoo, then, I'd sooner bear my peärt,
> Ov all the trials vo'k do rue,
> Than have a deadness o' the heart,
> Wi' nothen mwore to veel or do.
>
> (P, 301)

"Moss" is a poem in which the moss evokes mood and memory.
The mood is a melancholy realization of the relentless process of
time; the memory is of the speaker's own childhood and of friends
and faces now gone forever. The moss, while regarded as a mate,
"lowly plant that loo'st, like me, / The shadow of the woodland
tree," is also seen as a warning:

> While there in youth,—the sweetest part
> Of life,—with joy—believing heart,
> They liv'd their own dear days, all fraught
> With incidents for after-thought
> In later life, when fancy brought
> The outline of some faded face
> Again to its forsaken place.
> Come winter moss, creep on, creep on
> And warn me of the time that's gone.
>
> (P, 671)

Nature provides the catalyst for abstraction in "The Lark." Here,
the speaker is a laborer who has taken his two sons with him into
the fields to play while he works. The young boys laugh and run
through the grass as a lark flies overhead and sings "mwore in heären
than a zight." As the worker rakes his hay, he notices his children:
one has stopped, has shaded his eyes, and is searching the skies for
the bird whose song he hears while the other searches the ground
for whatever treasures he can find. The father is struck by the scene
and tries to sum up his thoughts in the last stanza:

> Zoo woone did watch above his head
> The bird his hands could never teäke;
> An' woone, below, where he did tread,

Vound out the nest within the breäke;
But, aggs be only woonce a-vound,
An' uncaught larks ageän mid [might] sound.

(*P,* 377)

The habits of birds in "Rooks and Swallows" makes an association in the mind of the poet with countervailing forces in the human psyche. These forces—the desire to quest after knowledge and action, and its opposite, the yearning for peace and stasis—are dealt with by other Victorians, perhaps most notably by Tennyson in "Ulysses" and "The Lotos Eaters," and by Matthew Arnold's "Stanzas From the Grand Chartreuse." The rooks, which are not migratory, represent those who, like Telemachus, stay home to guard order, peace, and orthodoxy. The swallows, on the other hand, migrate seeking a better climate when the winter winds blow, representing those adventurers who desire "To follow knowledge like a sinking star." The speaker here is torn both ways. Naturally, a linguist-historian-poet like Barnes would be drawn to the life of the knowledge-seeking traveler; but the teacher-priest was also attracted to his home fields and the tending of his flocks. The poem ends with a stanza which comments on the life he chose:

But since we lack the wings of gold
That waft men over all the earth,
And find our livelihood withhold
Our life to this our land of birth;
So let it be, since like a dove
We find us here enough to love.

(*P,* 745)

Perhaps the clearest expression of Barnes's conception of nature as the manifestation of God occurs in his poem, "Nature." Here, nature is described as a "Mysterious world that com'st between / Our yearning souls and God unseen"; but if nature serves as a barrier between the mortal and the transcendental, it also serves as a connection.

I seem to hear Him as I tread
Below the dead-leav'd beech's head,
Now rustling in the wind that flies
Ice-chilly from the eastern skies. . . .

Thus God is immanent in nature and as such is perceivable at those special times when man is attuned to natural processes and phenomena. At these special moments, glimpses of the other world are possible, Barnes says; like Hopkins in "God's Grandeur," he knows that when conditions are right, God's glory will "flame out, like shining from shook foil." At this moment, Barnes says, we are more certain about the Creator's purpose and more willingly accept Divine Providence:

> For land and stream, and rock and wood,
> Are as we see them for our good;
> Nor could our little wisdom mend
> What e'er a loving Good may send;
> Though the beginning and the end
>   Of blessings that may sometimes seem
>   But ills, are hidden in His scheme
> Of ever-teeming nature.
>
> (P, 638)

Nature, then, is the expression of God's will; that is why Barnes, like Hopkins and Wordsworth, reveres it and that is why he looks to the natural world in order to understand the mysteries of the supernatural one.

Religious Poetry

As a member of the clergy, it was natural for Barnes to write poetry which is religious in nature. The religious poems can be described as being homiletic or liturgical; in addition, Barnes wrote a drama in verse, "Ruth, A Short Drama From the Bible."

The homiletic poems are verses written on religious subjects which illustrate a theological or ethical point or elucidate a scriptural passage. A good example of the illustrative homiletic verse is "The Railroad," divided into two parts, each of which demonstrate Barnes's scientific as well as his religious interests. Part 1 begins with a description of how a person, when traveling across the terrain in a swiftly moving conveyance such as a railroad train, receives two distinct visual impressions. One is the sensation that objects close to the observer are flashing past; the other is that celestial objects much further away, like the sun, seem to travel along with the observer. Barnes uses this familiar visual phenomenon in a metaphor in which the scenery flashing by is compared to the passage of time, and the seeming constancy of the sun is compared to the presence of God in our lives:

> An' zoo, while time, vrom stage to stage,
> Do car [carry] us on vrom youth to age,
> The e'thly [earthly] pleasures we do vind
> Be soon a-met, an' left behind;
> But God, beholden vrom above
> Our lowly road, wi' yearnen love,
> Do keep bezide us, stage by stage,
> Vrom be'th to youth, vrom age to age.
>
> (P, 309)

"The Railroad," part 2, is similar in its structure and intent. Here, the traveler, when passing a park, trains his eye on a single distinctive oak tree within the grove. As the carriage moves on, all the other trees seem to wheel around the oak. Barnes uses this phenomenon to construct a metaphor in which the oak represents the single purpose which should be the center of concentration for each good Christian. Everything else—especially "e'thly pleasures"—must wheel about this single point:

> Zoo while our life do last, mid nought
> But what is good an' deär be sought,
> In word or deed, or heart or thought,
> An' all the rest wheel round it.
>
> (P, 310)

Mr. Collins, the character introduced in "The Leady's Tower," appears in some of the religious poems, "The Thorns in the Geate," for example, and "Good Measter Collins." In the former, the kindly clergyman joins a group of farm folk who have climbed a hill to view the progress of the newly sown grain. The speaker recounts how the fields have been plowed, rolled, and harrowed, the seed planted, and the bird boys assigned to protect the seed with shrill voices and clackers. Now, he says, the corn is "up ancle high" and all there is to do is to wait for harvest, trusting in providence and the weather. A row of thorny wood has been placed in the gate to ward off cattle from the young tender blades of grain. Mr. Collins comments on the thorns in the gate, placed there to insure that the corn will be unmolested during the ripening process, then takes the opportunity to deliver a religious message to the assemblage. The grain situation parallels the human one, the preacher says. Just as the farmer, once his planting is done, must trust in God for the fate of his corn, so must the Christian, once his or her religious duty is done, trust in God for the fate of the soul.

> in life let us vulvil [fulfill]
> Whatever is our Meäker's will,
> An' then bide still, wi' peacevul breast,
> While He do manage all the rest.
>   (P, 355)

The gifts of God—the only valuable ones, he says—are free and distributed equally to all His children.

Barnes wrote a series of six verses which he called "Sabbath Lays." These homiletic poems are numbered but untitled, and each is introduced by a scriptural quotation except for number 4. The poems then provide a commentary on the biblical message. Numbers 3 and 4, for example, present contrasting thoughts on the question "Why hast thou forsaken me?" from Mark 15:34.

Number 3 is a prayer from one who is on the verge of despair, who cries out to his maker for some sign of recognition or relief. The persona feels "cut off from human ways" and "number'd with the dead." He asked if this pain is sent to purify him as "silver in the fire." The question, written in the year of Gerard Manley Hopkins's birth, parallels a question that poet asks years later in the poem known as "Carrion Comfort." Hopkins asks, "Why wouldst thou rude on me / Thy wring-world right foot rock?" In both poems, too, the process of purgation is compared to the threshing of wheat, the separating of grain from chaff, and in both cases the rod of God is accepted as chief authority. Barnes describes his condition thus: "my soul in fear and pain / Is peaceless as the sea," while Hopkins also describes suffering and dread like a sailor in a storm: "O in turns of tempest, me heaped there; me frantic to avoid thee and flee?" The only vision of God Barnes's persona sees is a fearful one. He is "Before Thy frowning face, O God!" just as Hopkins's persona in the third stanza of "The Wreck of the Deutschland" sees "The frown of his face / Before me." The Hebrew words *Lama Sabachthani* are used as a refrain at the ends of each of the three stanzas; the issue is not resolved until we read lay number 4, which presents the soul as having passed out of its trial, now imbued with fresh faith.

Barnes's liturgical poems are written for specific church occasions; even the hymns celebrate particular activities, for example, a club service and harvest thanksgiving. Other liturgical poems were meant to be recited at services like baptisms, marriages, or church openings, with the poem's purpose stated in the title. Most of these are simple and conventional, aimed as they are at a conservative country audience. We can get a hint from many of these, however, why Barnes was so beloved in his native Dorset; he obviously turned his poetic talents to use in his church, honoring the recipients of holy sacraments from time to time not only with the rites that he was bound to give as a minister of God, but with the gift of his literary talent as well.

"Ruth, A Short Drama From the Bible" is a play in verse written for the parish stage. It is a fictionalized account of the Bible story, meant for both entertainment and instruction and supported by a choir singing psalms. Barnes keeps close to his source, explaining esoteric references in the stage directions for the benefit of the cast or in the dialogue for the audience. One is reminded of the medieval dramatic pageants of which Barnes was doubtless aware; the author even appends an epilogue to the play in the manner of the doctor's concluding speech in many of the biblical plays of the Middle Ages. Like the epilogues in the early dramas, Barnes intends that the message of the play be explicit as possible. He writes, "The history of Ruth shows the blessings of God on true-hearted love and kindness. From her faithfulness to Naomi she became a foremother of Kings David and Solomon; and in David and his offspring of the manhood of the Son of man" (*P*, 619).

The religious poetry is easily read and easily understood; it is appropriate to its audience in that it is written in simple language, it relates to the problems members of his parish would be likely to encounter, and it uses metaphors and images that persons of that place and time would readily identify or even use themselves.

Dorset Tales

As interested as he is in language and the oral tradition, it is no wonder that Barnes takes as subject matter for his own poetry the folk tales and legends of his native Dorset. As one might expect, most of these are told in the dialect, an attempt, no doubt, at retaining as much of the original flavor of the local legends as possible. Some of the tales seem peculiar to the region, while others are adaptations of stories told in other times and other places as well as in Dorset. In addition, Barnes tells some tales which seem to be his own fictional creations.

A good example of the pure Dorset tale is the one concerning the building of a church in one of the small communities of the region. This poem, "The Beam in Grenley Church," recounts the story of a strange man who worked with the laborers building the structure. He is described as being meek, cheerful, and strong—so strong

> that all alwone,
> He lifted beams an' blocks o' stwone,
> That others, with the girtest païns,
> Could hardly wag wi' bars an' chaïns;
> An' yet he never used to staÿ
> O' Zadurdays, to teäke his paÿ.
>
> (P, 203)

The rest of the men took little note of their volunteer companion until the morning after a particularly exasperating day. All day the men had worked hard hewing timbers and fitting blocks of stone; but late in the day, perhaps out of sheer exhaustion, a beam was cut too short to fit the structure, causing the men to leave the beam and retire for the night. The next morning when the crew returned to work, they found the beam not on the ground where they had left it, but in position high on the walls, somehow now the correct length. The stranger was nowhere to be seen, nor did he appear in the area ever again. There is much speculation among the people "whether he mid be a man / Or angel, wi' a helpen han', / Or whether all o't wer a dream" (P, 204), but the truth of the matter was never discovered. The story lives on in local legend and is perpetuated by Barnes's use of it in his poem.

Other local legends include those involving witches and fairies. An eclogue aptly named "The Veairies [fairies]" depicts a conversation between two Dorset locals, Simon and Samel, who are discussing the appearance of circular patterns in the grassland vegetation that the local population have named "fairy rings." There are two theories, Simon says, about what causes the phenomenon—lightning or the tracks left by fairies as they dance in their nocturnal festivities. The local system of beliefs concerning the little people is then explored, from the instruments used to produce music at the fairy ball—

> There's nar a fiddle that's a-heär'd at all;
> But they do plaÿ upon a little pipe,
> A-meäde o' kexes [stems of hemlock or cow parsley]
>   or o' straws, dead ripe,
> A-stuck in row (zome short an' longer zome)
> Wi' slime o' snaïls, or bits o' plum-tree gum,—

to the kinds of dance steps they use—"jigs to fit their little veet," not "The dree an' vow'r han' [three and four hand] reels that we do sprawl / An' kick about in" (*P,* 134).

The eclogue entitled "A Ghost" recounts many of the ghost stories of the Dorset countryside in much the same manner. Jem and Dick, the two speakers, are walking together on a dark evening and naturally enough begin to talk about the various apparitions that have been sighted over the years in their locality. They compare notes on the poltergeist which haunts a particular house, changing shapes ranging from a six-feet tall model in white with burning coals for eyes to a smileless lady dressed in silk, all the while slamming doors and moving furniture in ghostly fashion. Dick then tells the story of Jack Hime who was returning home after an all-night party at which he "mid a-took a cup / Or two o' eäle [ale] a-keepen Chris'mas up" when he came upon a great dog on the road. Intending to send the dog home to its master, Jack took a stick in his hand and began to beat the animal; instead of hitting it, though, the stick broke into four pieces which then flew over his head and came down to stick into the ground at the four points of the compass. Jack's hand got numb, his arm began to swell, and later his skin began to peel, proving once again that strange dogs should be left to lie whether they are sleeping or not. In addition to this obvious truth, Barnes no doubt repeated the story as a bit of a temperance lecture, even if the force of this is lost on Dick and Jem (*P,* 184–86).

As an example of the ubiquitous folk story, versions of which are told in many cultures, Barnes offers the dramatic monologue "A Witch," wherein the narrator whispers gossip to a companion concerning Molly Brown, a neighbor who is passing by. The speaker alleges that Molly is a witch who possesses the evil eye, and denies that the old woman is being defamed by lies and made-up stories. He or she then goes on to tell a story—one which the speaker has heard repeated—concerning Molly and Farmer Gruff's family, how the Gruffs denied a request to borrow some unremembered object, and how they were rewarded by a series of misfortunes allegedly brought forth by the woman's "pow'r." The Gruff's milk and ale turned "zour," the "aggs" addled, and the cheese turned back to curds and whey, reversing several natural chemical reactions in the process; the animals all got sick or, like the little pigs, "turned their snouts [or noses, or bills] to the sky," "gave a little grunt [or bray, or quack], and died." All efforts to stop the curse, including nailing a horseshoe over the farmhouse door and ostracizing Molly, proved fruitless. Finally, the farmer's wife, in an apparent attempt at a countercharm, tried to draw blood from Molly's body by "dawking" needles and pins through "her wold hard wither'd skin." Even this failed, the narrator says, because the sharp instruments all broke before piercing the old lady's hide; in fact, this last operation had the opposite of its intended effect since it "Did meäke the hag bewitch em woo'se" (*P*, 224–25).

Of course, the Gruff's cruelty to the old woman is not lost to the reader even if it is to the narrator. Through his skillful reporting of this speech, Barnes shows that he is capable of producing all the subtle irony that the dramatic monologue is famed for. His skill in exposing small-minded rural hypocrisy through the use of dramatic forms and dialect speech was admired by his countryman Thomas Hardy. Hardy's "The Ruined Maid" is a good example of his emulation of Barnes in this regard.

Another universal tale Barnes tells is that of "The Weepen Leady," a variation of a folk story told in many places around the world at many different times. The legend tells of a weeping lady who at certain times haunts an old house. The figure that appears on moonlit nights is believed by the natives to be that of a woman long dead. The woman had given birth to a son out of wedlock, leading her father to offer her two equally dreadful alternatives: either she must leave that country forever, or her son must be sent away "a thousand mile." The lady, Barnes reports, chose to leave herself and "Left the hwome ov all her pride / To wander drough the worold wide / Wi' grief that vew but she ha' tried." Later, "she wither'd wi' the

deadly stroke" and died; now she returns to her formerly happy
home

> To zee her father dead and gone,
> As if her soul could have noo rest
> Avore her teary cheäk's a-prest
> By his vorgiven kiss.
>
> (*P*, 171)

Thus Barnes treats the often repeated tale of the woman whose
restless spirit is doomed to return to familiar earthly scenes until
whatever is bothering it is removed. England has several of these
female apparitions, variously given names like the "Green Lady"
and the "Lady with the Lantern;" even northeastern Wisconsin has
its "Lady in Red."

While Barnes uses familiar folk tales as material for his work, he
sometimes creates fictions of his own as well. The subtitle to his
"Erwin and Linda" is given as "A Tale of Tales." The poem is not
a retelling of a preexistent folktale, but rather the poet's attempt
at spinning a yarn using a *Decameron*-type of setting. The first verse
paragraph—written as is most of the rest of the poem in iambic
pentameter couplets—sets up the scene: several neighbors have gathered for a winter's evening before a warm fire "Each ready as his
turn might come, to hold / The others' minds with tales as yet
untold."

Mrs. Fanny begins with her tale of Erwin's childhood. If it were
not for Barnes's subtitles—"Mrs. Fanny's Tale," "Mr. John's Tale,"
etc.—the seven narrators would be indistinguishable from one another. Each in turn picks up the thread of the story, continues for
an episode, and passes it on. The tale is a well-worn one, involving
an orphan boy who is tricked out of his inheritance, but who through
good-natured hard work, thrift, and even some heroics, manages to
regain his fortune along with the hand of a girl he has long worshipped from afar but has been afraid to approach because of his
reduced circumstances. The story is complete with a profligate brother
who foolishly spends his and Erwin's inheritance and a villain named
Wingreed who does his best to thwart Erwin's climb back to
respectability.

We can guess that "Erwin and Linda" was originally written as
a children's story purely for entertainment. Bernard Jones reports

in his notes to the poem that fragments of the manuscript show that the hero was at first not named Erwin, but rather Egbert, the name of Barnes's younger son. Further, there is a distinct lack of subtlety about the poem. It is fast-paced and full of action with two rescue scenes—one involving a flood, the other a fire. There is a simple, clear moral tying in with the defeat of the bad guys by the good guys at the end. Finally, the episodic nature of the poem makes it very conducive to reading to children at bedtime.

Homely Rhymes

The term "homely rhymes" is one Barnes uses himself to designate verses written to describe the rural life and to depict its day-to-day occupations, reminiscences of country childhood, customs and holidays in the rural shires, rustic humor, and plain, honest country wisdom. It was his conservationist tendencies as much as anything else which prompted these poems. Barnes probably had two major specific aims for these works, the first being simply the recording of English rural life before it was buried under the landslide of time and change which he knew to be threatening his peaceful Dorset valleys. The second aim was more didactic. Barnes wished to portray the simple country life as an exemplar for Victorian society. He saw that the way out of many of the social, political, and spiritual dilemmas of the day was for people to turn back to the old values and traditions, to those attributes which were still practiced and preserved in pockets of English countryside.

Some of these poems deal with rural occupations and agricultural practices; at times, Barnes even seems to be following the example of the classical georgic, in which directions in or descriptions of specific tasks are given. The poet knew Hesiod's *Works and Days* and Virgil's *Georgics* and was no doubt impressed by their emphasis on the dignity of labor and their praise of the simple country life. The dialect poem "Vellen O' the Tree" is a good example of a description of a specific task. The speaker first describes the tree as it was before being approached by the cutters, remembering how it provided shade and a resting place for mowers.

Then the approach of the felling crew and its operations are described. First, a rope is attached "At the top o'n, wi' woone end a-hanged to ground," and a cut is made "near the ground" until "his girt [great] stem a'most drough." At this point, the crew leaves off its cutting, and all the men begin to tug at the rope, dictating the direction of fall. Giving in to the pressures above and below, the tree "swayëd all his limbs, an' he nodded his head, / Till he vell away down like a pillar o' lead" (*P*, 183). Some sadness is expressed for the passing of the great tree as well as awe for its enormous size on the ground. Stanza one deals with the tree as it was in the past while providing a concise, specific description of the mowers' occupation and appurtenances. Stanza 2, on the other hand, treats the subject of the tree in the present while providing the reader with a description of the craft of tree-cutting.

"Hay-Meaken" and "Hay-Carren," too, are in the georgic mode, being descriptions of those processes which their titles suggest. Again, the descriptions are quite specific in the manner of Virgil's instructions on grafting fruit trees in book 2 of the *Georgics*. In "Hay-Carren," for example, the proper method of loading hay onto a wagon is given.

> The bwoy is at the hosse's head,
> An' up upon the waggon bed
> The lwoaders, strong o' eärm do stan',
> At head, an' back at taïl, a man,
> Wi' skill to build the lwoad upright
> An' bind the vwolded corners tight;
> An' at each zide o'm, sprack [lively] and strong,
> A pitcher wi' his long-stemmed prong.
>
> (P, 116)

Haying is the subject of another occupational poem, the eclogue entitled "The Best Man in the Vield," in which two haymakers argue about who is better at his work. Other specialties are treated, too, in poems such as "The Milk-Maid O' the Farm," "Fiddler Bob," and "Thatchen O' the Rick." These poems, perhaps again showing the influence of Virgil, offer panegyrics to country life, recognizing that in it lies what remains of the golden age.

The brightest gold, though, belongs to the child growing up in the countryside. Barnes's poetry contains many reminiscences of children's games, of solitary explorations of nature during boyhood, and of other youthful experiences. "Grammer's Shoes" and "The Settle and the Girt Wood Vire" are good examples of childhood memories preserved in poetry. The first poem describes how the children used to gather around their grandmother at Christmas time begging her to open her chest of ancient treasures to show her wedding shoes and dress. This was done to the accompaniment of stories "O' the merry wold soul how she did use / To laugh an' to dance wi' her high-heel shoes." The second poem, too, features a speaker who remembers similar simple country pleasures. He addresses a friend who had been his companion as a boy, and asks if he remembers the great fireplaces and mantles the houses had when they were young. He compares the old settle, its bacons curing and bags of herbs drying alongside great racks of plates and pewterware, with the newer version:

> a little hole
> To tëake a little greäte o' coal,
> So small that only twos or drees
> Can jist push in an' warm their knees.
>
> (*P*, 174)

The childhood poems extol the virtues of country living while they recognize and exclaim against the changes which were occurring in agricultural communities all across England. These things are true, too, about the homely rhymes which Barnes writes about the customs and holidays of the rural Dorset communities. The traditional holidays are treated in poems like "Easter Zunday," "Keepen Up O' Christmas," and "Guy Faux's Night," but the local holidays are not ignored. In the two "Shrodon Feair" poems, the narrator relates the events surrounding that rural celebration, the country fair. The first poem describes the excitement of the people as they ready themselves—"Dick and I did brush our hats / An' cwoats, an' clean ourzelves lik' cats"—and the arrival at "Shrodon seäfe and sound / Astrutten in among the rows / O' tilted stannes [market stalls] an' o' shows." The speaker tries to capture the atmosphere of the fair through his description:

> An' girt long booths wi' little bars,
> Chock'vull o' barrels, mugs, and jars . . .
> Where zellers bwold to buyers shy
> Did hollow round us, "What d'ye buy?" . . .
> An' horns did blow, an' drums did rumble,
> An' bawlen merrymen did tumble. . . .
>
> (*P*, 154)

The second Shrodon Fair poem continues with the description of the fair, the characters meeting friends from other districts, shaking dice for a gingerbread treat, and returning home. Barnes's careful attention to detail in his depictions of what he saw to be a rural institution endangered by modernization indicates that he was attempting to preserve the memory of this important social event.

But Barnes writes of less convivial customs than attending fairs, the keeping of Christmas, and "Zitten Out the Wold Year." "Leady-Day an' Ridden House" describes the all too common scene in which a farm family loses its lease and is forced to leave for another location. Lady Day, 25 March, ends the first quarter of the new year. As such, it was traditionally the day on which yearly leases ran out, necessitating the removal of tenants, or "ridden house." The speaker in this poem gives all the details of his melancholy task, providing the reader with a veritable catalog of nineteenth-century household goods: firedogs, copper kettles, the butter-barrel and cheese wring, the salt box, as well as miscellaneous chairs and stools. The poem ends with the old wagon loaded and the family waiting while the speaker makes one last round, checking "In fusty holes an' darksome nooks, / To gather all I still mid vind." He confesses sadness at leaving "the he'th / An' ruf" that once made him happy, and does not linger long in the now deserted house. The poem closes with his stoic comment, "Zoo ridden house is such a caddle [confusing plight], /That I would rather keep my staddle" (*P,* 75). A staddle is the set of footings upon which the hayrick sits; in the farmer's mind, it is the symbol of the stable axis of the farm, much as the hearth is seen as the center of the household. The "caddle" of the situation, of course, is not just the confusion surrounding moving household goods, but the loss of equilibrium which accompanies such uprootings. Barnes's sympathetic treatment of this subject is such that one might dare say that ridden house was not one of the country customs he was intent on preserving.

Most of the subjects of the homely rhymes, though, are happy ones. He sees generally that these folk customs are important in that they provide both stability and continuity to the lives of the people. Poems like "Harvest Hwome"—a description of the great feasts which traditionally follow a cooperatively brought in harvest—and "Minden House"—a demonstration of the practice of petitioning the father for a young woman's hand in marriage—give the reader an indication of the central role custom and tradition played in the rural society Barnes was writing about.

Dialect literature has long been used as a source of humor. Chaucer himself makes effective use of dialect to produce laughter in the "Miller's Tale" and elsewhere; dialect humor continues in the English and American literary traditions, reaching a peak during the nineteenth century. Barnes does not overlook this use of local speech; much of his work contains good-natured humor.

The eclogue "A Bit O' Sly Coorten" is an example of one kind of humor to which lovers are so often prone. Here John has waited for Fanny arriving late for their meeting and is further put out by her attentions to another man. Fanny, for her part, plays John's jealousy for all that it is worth and, while feigning innocence, cunningly fuels the fire with lines like "If he kiss'd me dree times, or a dozen, / What harm wer it? Why idden [isn't] he my cousin?"(P, 96).

Practical jokes have their appeal to some, and Barnes uses these as subjects for his humorous verse, too. In "Polly Be-en Upzides Wi' Tom," the female speaker tells how she, in the best tradition of Sut Lovingood, the American prankster, found Tom Dumpy's coat where he had removed it in order to do some work. Polly confesses to taking the coat, sewing shut the sleeves and collar, and then returning it to where its owner had left it. A group of young people subsequently gathered to watch Tom try to put on the garment when he came in from the field; the company, of course, laughed uproariously at his misfortune. By the end of the poem, Polly tells the boy to whom she has given such attention that she hopes he has learned his lesson; she says she hopes he's learned

> He mussen [mustn't] think to peck
> Upon a body zoo, nor whip
> The meäre to drow me off, nor tip
> Me out o' cart ageän, nor slip
> Cut hoss-heäir down my neck.
>   (P, 128)

Practical jokes other than those of the adolescent romance are depicted as well. In "What Dick and I Did," the speaker tells of two boys who are resentful at not being asked to attend a "randy," or party, at the Brown's house. As a result, they sabotage the gathering. Just when the party has reached its height, the pair take a small grinding stone and use it to stop up the chimney. Those inside scamper out while the delighted jokers watch:

> The maïdens cough'd or stopped their breath,
> The men did hauk and spet
> The wold vo'k bundled out from he'th
> Wi' eyes a-runnen wet.

> (P, 167)

Riddles, too, are among the subjects for the humorous poems; the dialogue poem "Riddles: Anne and Joey A-Ta'ken" is one of these. Here, two country people try to stump one another with riddles such as this one describing a wheelbarrow.

> A two lagg'd thing do run avore
> An' run behind a man,
> An' never run upon his lags
> Though on his lags do stan'.

Barnes's humor is usually gentle, but at times his wit is barbed, as when he gives us the wonderful situational comedy of "The Waggon A-Stooded." Here, the rustics who have allowed a loaded wagon to become stuck in the mud are depicted as buffoons, shouting orders and recriminations at one another, and generally behaving like Keystone Cops. "Gruffmoody Grim" paints an exaggerated picture of the local grouch in which Barnes makes fun of all bad-humored people.

The homely rhymes as a group, though, are intended to demonstrate some simple truths; the dignity of work, the innate wisdom and intelligence of the poor but honest farmer, and the superiority of the country life. In "The Lew O' the Rick," for example, a farmer sits with his haystack shielding him on a cold and windy evening, his mind "in vaïceless thought." He surveys his little world, his musings turning to eternity and his place in it. "Tweil [Toil]" is a similar poem representing a farmer's thoughts on work. He sees labor as what gives structure and substance to his life. What threatens him is not toil or its inevitability, but rather the chance that he might be deprived of the opportunity to work.

The importance of the past, of recognizing the value of past works and deeds, is demonstrated in "Our Father's Works." Here, the speaker describes the works of former generations, the bridges that were built, the ground that was cleared, the structures that were erected. The speaker, in a statement which is indicative of Barnes's philosophy, entreats the reader not to neglect the lessons of the past.

> Zoo now mid nwone ov us vorget
> The pattern our vorefathers zet;
> But each be faïn to underteäke
> Zome work to meäke vor others' gaïn,
> That we mid leäve mwore good to sheäre,
> Less ills to bear, less souls to grieve,
> An' when our hands do vall to rest,
> It mid be vrom a work a-blest.
>
> (*P, 270*)

The homely rhymes are representative of all of Barnes's poetry, indeed, of all of his work. They are learned, yet simple, sensible, yet compassionate, and while they appeal to a wider audience, are addressed to the simple country folk who make up their substance. They are full of hope, confidence, grace, and good cheer. While those attributes might be considered gauche in our modern poetry, it is yet refreshing to look back to a time when the possibility of an uncomplicated, essentially happy society was held out.

Chapter Three
Philological and Linguistic Works

The Philological Climate

Barnes's study of linguistics and philology has its roots in eighteenth-century philosophy; in many ways he was to continue the work of earlier English and continental philologists who regarded the study of language as a necessary but ancillary activity to investigations into philosophy. But Barnes was a "new" philologist, too, in spite of his relative isolation from the universities and centers of population. He was adept at preserving what was valuable from older systems and ideas while at the same time eager to put new theses and propositions to the test. For these reasons a review of the major issues and concerns of language scholars during the late eighteenth and early nineteenth centuries is necessary for an understanding of Barnes's philological activities.

Most eighteenth-century philosopher-linguists believed that language is the outward manifestation of the mind, that language is invented by the mind, and that it operates according to the same principles as the mind. Therefore, they thought, an explanation of how language operates and a description of what it is helps to explain and describe the mind itself. This reasoning is at the heart of eighteenth-century philology.

Along with this philosophic bent, philology in the eighteenth century took a more rational and scientific turn than it had shown before. This was a reflection of what was happening in almost every field of intellectual endeavor: all branches of learning were receiving heavy amounts of fall-out from the Newtonian explosion. Linguists were reluctant to accept the authority of older grammarians and theorists—both ancient and modern—and sought to order their thinking on empirical evidence.

Attempts were made during this time to compile a universal grammar which would apply equally to all languages. These attempts were based on the idea that language is the manifestation, even a picture or copy, of the mind. Since the mind itself, in its essential nature, is universal to all human beings, by extension all languages are alike in the important ways. Basically, the universal grammarians asserted, all languages have a common structure, although they do differ in several obvious respects. A universal grammar would be one, they said, that states all general linguistic principles which each grammar of a particular language must demonstrate. A famous attempt at compiling such a universal grammar was made in 1660 by Claude Lancelot and Antoine Arnauld. Their *Grammaire general et raisonee,* also known as the *Port-Royal Grammar* and as *L'art de parler,* was a major work whose influences lasted until the end of the eighteenth century. While this work used only Latin and French to illustrate their principles, the authors claimed that they would apply as well to any language. The influence of the *Port-Royal Grammar* is apparent in the work of many philologists who followed Lancelot and Arnauld. These Port Royal grammarians, as they came to be called, attempted to arrive at a general grammar by closely examining Latin, Greek, and Hebrew, as well as the modern European languages, to show basic underlying principles common to all. These linguists, through their studies of the modern European languages, lent a legitimacy to the study of vernacular tongues which therefore had been enjoyed only by the study of classical languages.[1]

Another concern of eighteenth-century philologists was the mystery surrounding the origin of language. While this was not a new issue—speculation on the beginnings of language has occurred throughout history—it did tend to give to linguistic studies an historical perspective that had not previously been emphasized. These philologists attempted to explain what lay between man's first attempts at speech and the relatively complex modern situation in which hundreds of languages exist side by side, albeit with common underlying principles. Such attempts gave impetus to the systematic historically based study of language which was to become prevalent in the nineteenth century.

Several philosopher-philologists of the eighteenth century made important contributions to the study of language, among them Etienne Bonnot de Condillac. His work helped to set the stage for the burst of philological activity which was to occupy Europe for much of the next century. Condillac's doctrine of signs attempted to account for the origin of human knowledge and for the operation of the mind, perennial subjects for discussion, especially in the eighteenth century. A follower of Locke, Condillac explained all thinking as arising from sensation and from man's response to his environment. He maintained, as did Rousseau, that language evolved from natural cries and imitative gestures; he asserted that the development of language and the development of thinking are interdependent, that man's attempts to respond to his environment led to more and more efficient methods of communication which led to greater ability to think and to rationalize which in turn led to better forms of communication, and so on. This process, according to Condillac, led to the development of language as we know it, as well as to man's relatively advanced mental capabilities, including reflection, memory, and imagination. Condillac's theory touches upon most of the areas of concern for eighteenth-century linguistics. He looked to the universal grammar, to the origin of language, and to the historical description of the development of language. The theory itself, it should be noted, was brought forward because of Condillac's belief that Locke's ideas on the origin of knowledge had not gone far enough; the French scholar was typically approaching philology as a branch of philosophy.

Condillac was only one of many scholars in the late eighteenth century who were grappling with the problem of explaining the origin of language. In 1796, the Prussian Academy offered a prize for an essay which would explain how man evolved his own language without the divine intervention espoused by many people. The Academy hoped to settle an argument between those who believed that speech evolved from animallike cries and gestures into the present-day organization of relatively complex languages by means of natural processes and those who believed that language is a direct gift to man from God. The latter used as their authority the Bible; the former attempted to apply a more rational, scientific methodology.

The Prussian Academy prize was awarded to J. G. Herder for his 1772 essay *Abhandlung über den Ursprung der Sprache*. Herder, like Condillac, asserted that language and the operation of the mind cannot be separated, that language is part of thinking, that thinking cannot exist without language. He saw that language and thought have a common origin. His essay stated that language came into being through a natural process, and that language is a tool, a facilitator of thought and reason. Herder went beyond the charge of the Academy in that he discussed more than the origin of language; his treatise was on the very nature of language and its development. He saw language as being an integral component of man, a part of his very nature, and one of the basic elements that make up the human being. The study of language drew Herder's attention, too. He maintained that a language could be studied like any organism, that its development could be traced from birth to maturity just as one would trace the life of an individual or the course of a nation's history. Language, like other organisms, is subject to natural laws, according to Herder, and operates according to certain principles which can be described by the philological scholar. Language and its development are inextricably bound to history itself; indeed, the study of the development of language is necessary to a full understanding of natural, social, and political history. Herder's ideas, like Condillac's, were influential, especially in Germany where the science of philology was beginning to burgeon.

In England, James Harris (1709–80) was approaching the study of language from another direction. Harris was an Aristotelian scholar who used Aristotle as the philosophic basis for his philological ideas. He was a leading exponent of the theory of universal grammar which saw that language, like all things, is governed by a set of underlying principles. No matter what the outward appearance of a particular language might be, no matter how different it might seem to be from some other tongue, the laws which govern it govern all languages and are immutable. Harris, as a universal grammarian, was interested in discovering and describing these principles, but he was also aware of the importance of studying the variations among languages. These he saw as being connected closely with the history, customs, and mores of the group of people to which a language belongs. Harris, like Herder, influenced the study of language in that he helped tie philology to the rising interest in natural history, ethnography, and nationalism. Barnes, as we will see, used his own philological studies to pursue questions in these areas as well.

Harris and another English philologist, James Burnett or Lord Monboddo (1714–99), were considered by many to be exemplars of the traditional philology, the "old" philology, which was to come under the attack of the "new" philology in the nineteenth century. Monboddo's philology, like that of many of his contemporaries, depended to a large extent on his particular brand of philosophy. His description of the origin of language, for instance, reflects his conception of man. He makes the distinction between man as a work of God—the natural, primitive being—and man as a work of man—the rational, advanced being. God provided the natural materials, human physiology and mental abilities, but man himself brought about the changes in himself which led to all those attributes and conditions called civilization. The study of the development of language is important to Monboddo because it is through the tracing of its history that we get an accurate picture of the history of civilization itself. In addition, because of his definition of language as "the expression of the conceptions of the mind by articulate sounds,"[2] Monboddo sees the development of language as a model of the progress of the human mind. He differs from many of his contemporaries in his assertion that the acquisition of language is not natural; rather, he says, it is a highly artificial process. This process, because of its intricacy, can only be mastered by man since he alone has the necessary mental equipment. This is not to say, however, that even speech itself is natural to man, Monboddo goes on, because just the contrary is true; language is an artifice, a highly advanced tool produced by man for his own use.

By the end of the eighteenth century, the historical approach to the study of language had increased in importance and was making significant contributions to scholarship. Until around the turn of the century, though, few attempts had been made to examine in detail many languages other than the classical and the modern European. When this situation began to change, when scholars began to look more to the East, many new advances were possible. In 1786, Sir William Jones opened a new era in philology when he delivered a paper to the Royal Asiatic Society in Calcutta. Jones's thesis was that Sanskrit, the classical language of the Indian subcontinent, shares a common source with Greek, Latin, and the Germanic languages.

The importance of this discovery lies not with the revelation itself as much as with the fact that Jones established direct links among various languages in terms of both structure and etymology. Further, the Jones statement came at a time when Europe's face was turned to the East. There was a new interest in India and the Near East partly precipitated by the Napoleonic Wars and Napoleon's personal interest in the area. The effect of Jones's announcement was to initiate a serious comparison of Sanskirt with the European languages studies, which in turn supported generally the growth of comparative linguistics based on historical principles. This led, too, to the rise of modern descriptive linguistics and to the study of Indian linguistic systems and theories. Perhaps the greatest contribution Jones made to the study of language was his providing of a focal point for scholars who were to follow. Many of the early historical linguists were Sanskrit scholars; their contributions in this one area led other philologists to build upon the work in Sanskrit and to make applications of these ideas in other language studies.

One of the Sanskrit scholars who became important to the science of philology was Freidrich von Schlegel. Schlegel began his study of Oriental languages in Paris during 1802. By 1808, he had produced his *Ueber die Sprache und Weisheit der Indier (On the Language and Learning of the Indians)*, a work which was influential in bringing a new methodology to language studies. Schlegel sought to encourage not only language studies, but historical studies in general; in fact, only about 25 percent of this work deals with language. In the book, he insists upon the importance of comparative grammar which helps to reveal a language's innermost structure and upon the scientific study of roots rather than the speculative construction of etymologies. He introduces the idea of drawing "family trees" for particular languages, adapting a methodology from biology to demonstrate the common source of and relationships among languages. His study of roots aids the search for an *Ursprache,* or common source, for modern languages because by examining the roots he is able to determine the comparative ages of languages. Schlegel divides languages into two main types, based on inner structure. He maintains that changes of meaning are marked either by inflection of the root or by the addition of a separate word. Since these two methods account for the change of meaning in all cases, Schlegel states that each language uses one system or the other; thus each language can be said to be inflectional or noninflectional. The author's brother, August Wilhelm von Schlegel, was also a scholar in Oriental languages. He became professor of literature at the University of Bonn in 1818; in this position, he was able to encourage and foster Indic studies in Germany for many years. Friedrich's book and Wilhelm's professorship were instrumental in charting the course of German philological scholarship through the nineteenth century.

Another important contributor to language studies in the early nineteenth century was Rasmus Rask. Rask's major influence came about through a work he produced in response to a prize offer made by the Danish Academy of Sciences in 1811. The topic proposed by the Academy was threefold: it asked contributors to determine the source from which the old Scandinavian language is derived; to describe the development of the language from the oldest periods, through the Middle Ages, to the present Nordic and Germanic dialects; and to put forth a set of precise principles for use when studying the languages. Rask's monograph, *An Investigation Concerning the Source of the Old Northern or Icelandic Language,* examined neighboring languages—Greenlandic Eskimo, Celtic, Basque, Finnish, Slavic, Lettish, Thracian (Rask's name for the ancestor of Latin and Greek, that is, Indo-European), and the Asiatic languages. This work was a comparative Indo-European grammar which helped give rise to the study of comparative Indo-European linguistics. The works of Rask and Grimm were pioneering efforts in the new philology.

Rask's *Investigation* was read by Jacob Grimm who used some of Rask's ideas in the formulation of his *Deutsche Grammatik,* or *Germanic Grammar.* With Rask and Grimm, the historical examination of the Indo-European language group began in earnest. Grimm's *Grammar* puts forth what has come to be called Grimm's Law, although this "law" is really a set of nine rules. These rules spell out the relationship of German consonants with those of Greek and other Indo-European languages and thus the relationships among the languages themselves. The grammar was the first comprehensive look at the ancient Indo-European vernacular and its offspring.[3]

While the "new" philology was prospering in Germany and Scandinavia, it was faring less well in England. In the 1830s and 1840s, though, language studies began to come into their own in Britain, largely through the efforts of Benjamin Thorpe and John Mitchell Kemble. Both were Old English scholars who has studied under Rask and Grimm in Europe, and it was mainly through these men that the new philological doctrines and methods were introduced to Britain. Until this time, to some degree because of the English universities' aversion to the new science, philology had been in the hands of amateurs, many of whom were influenced by Horne Tooke. For much of the remainder of the century, language studies continued to be done by interested individuals rather than by academicians, but this situation was made tolerable by the learned societies, most notable the Philological Society of London.[4]

Tooke's influence was pervasive in early nineteenth-century England. His *Epea Pteroenta or the Diversions of Purley* took Harris to task rather vociferously. Tooke saw the origin of language as being derived from natural animal cries and asserted that these cries survived in the language as interjections. Language evolved, he asserted, as interjections eroded into other forms. These new forms came about because of the natural tendency in all language to run smoothly. Only two parts of speech were admitted to Tooke's grammar, the nouns and verbs. As proof for his theories, Tooke constructed detailed etymologies, a common practice for linguists of the old school. As it turns out, however, many of these etymologies were more imaginative than accurate, as was the case much of the time. At the heart of Tooke's philology is the assertion that all words ultimately are names for sensations; this thesis depends to a large degree not on linguistic scholarship as much as on Tooke's philosophy. Since many intellectuals in England—notably the Utilitarians— were of the same philosophical persuasion as Tooke, they also accepted his philology. This symbiotic combination was hard to dislodge, and Tooke's theories dominated English language studies until the 1840s.

By 1842, however, Kemble and Thorpe had infused English studies with the new philological theories and methodologies of the Germans and Scandinavians. In this year, Edwin Guest convened the first meeting of a group that came to be called the Philological Society of London. This group, led by Guest, and later by Frederick Furnivall, James A. H. Murray, and others, provided sorely needed leadership in the area of language studies in England. The Society undertook many worthwhile projects, including the monumental task of compiling the *Oxford English Dictionary* which turned out to be one of the most important philological projects in history. This dictionary defines words on historical principles, the methodology of the "new" philology.[5]

When Barnes came upon the scene, then, conditions were ripe for the blossoming of linguistics study. Important advances were just beginning to be made on the Continent; in England, the old wordlist methodology was starting to give way to the newer, more scientific approaches. Further, philology was tied closely with ethnography and with natural history, two very popular topics in the nineteenth century, not only with academicians and intellectuals, but also with the general public. In many ways, nationalism and evolution dominated the thinking of the time, and philology was closely linked to both.

Barnes as a Philologist

Barnes had an early interest in languages, having studied French and Italian with his friend Edward Fuller while they were both young bachelors in Dorchester. In fact, when Barnes moved from Dorchester to Mere, the two young men corresponded in French so as not to lose what they had learned. Most of the subsequent language training Barnes received was self-taught. Early on, he got some informal tutoring, such as that from friendly clergymen Lane Fox and the Reverend Mr. Richman, both of whom offered books and lessons, but for the most part the budding linguist studied on his own. He seemed to have a knack for learning languages; too, as a teacher he was always looking for the best pedagogical tools for teaching languages. By putting his teaching interests and natural talents together, he was able to acquire fluency in a number of ancient and modern tongues.

Barnes's interest in philology was given a boost when he left his law clerkship in Dorchester to become a schoolmaster in the neighboring town of Mere. Barnes was hired to take over Mr. Robertson's school, an opportunity that the young man took so that he might improve his financial position to the point where he might marry Julia Miles. The vocational change did call for some little sacrifice on his part, though; the new teacher had to work hard on his class preparation, and he had to do it alone, for Julia was to remain in Dorchester until just before their marriage in 1827. Barnes used his four years well by plunging deeply into philological studies. His notebooks and diaries tell us that he continued his studies in French and Italian while also turning to Latin, Greek, and German. In these languages—especially in French—he was given some help from Charles Masson, a French naval surgeon who had been brought to England as a prisoner of war, had subsequently married an Englishwoman, and had settled down to live at Mere. The two became friends and conversed at length in French. To help himself improve in German and Italian, Barnes began keeping daily diaries in these languages. Recognizing the importance of learning non-European tongues, the young teacher was able to find a grammar and to begin his study of Persian. Persian was to play an important part in both his poetical practice and his philological ideas, but the study of Russian, also started about this time, was aborted early.

In 1827, William and Julia were married and moved into an old rambling house near the local church. Before the Reformation it had been used as a priest's house, or chantry, and this name was still used when the couple moved in. The study of language continued in Chantry House, where Barnes took up Hebrew and Hindustani; in the early 1830s he took up the study of Welsh language and literature, an avocation which was to last for the rest of his life. He began at this time to compose poetry in Italian, turning out sonnets in the style of Petrarch, one of his favorite poets. His interest now began to turn to the serious study of philological theory, and he soon published a paper called "Linguiana" in the *Dorset County Chronicle.* The article is an etymological study of some English words of Latin and Greek derivation. In 1829, he published *An Etymological Glossary of English Words of Foreign Derivation, So Arranged That the Learner is Enabled to Acquire the Meaning of Many at Once.* The aim of this short work is pedagogical as the title indicates; it is also indicative of the writer's continuing interest in the history of language. The work itself is a list of words which have entered English from other languages, providing historical evidence for various etymological changes. His affiliation with the *Gentlemen's Magazine* began in 1831 with the publication of several articles on philological subjects which demonstrate how his attention was turning to language theory. In this year he published essays on English derivatives, on the structure of dictionaries, on the pronunciation of Latin, and on hieroglyphics.

W. D. Jacobs, in his work *William Barnes, Linguist,* asserts that Barnes's linguistic works "are of real value to students of language and literature on at least six counts."[6] First of all, he says that Barnes's general theory of language is rich and exciting, that while perhaps some of it can be rejected in the light of modern linguistic scholarship, it cannot be overlooked or dismissed. Second, Barnes's insistence on a return to purity in the English language goes far beyond any of his predecessors; no one has gone as far as he in challenging the Latinization of English in both theory and practice. Too, Barnes's ideas about the purity of the language constitute a real possibility for reform in that they contain an actual program of action. Fourth, as part of this program, Barnes puts forth hundreds of word revivals, conversions, and neologisms based on Old English. Many of these have now entered normal usage with no credit being given to their reviver. Another important element of Barnes's philology is his actual practice when writing his works; they are written with a native vocabulary, that is, one from which most foreign elements have been removed. His prose, especially in his later works, consists almost entirely of words of Anglo-Saxon derivation. It is theory being tempered with the fire of practice. Jacobs's sixth point is that Barnes's work constitutes the largest set of argument against the Latinization of English.

This part of Barnes's philology—his insistence on the return to a Saxon-English language, as he called it—was based at least to some degree on his social theory. (Perhaps we can detect here that eighteenth-century bent of mind in which the philology must fit the philosophy.) The man spent his entire life in rural England, ministering to the intellectual and spiritual needs of the common people, families of generations of yeoman farmers, clans of simple tradesmen. The English language, he maintained, must be understood by the common people and must be the basis for emotional appeals to these people, such as appeals of religion, patriotism, or altruism: "We should not reach the English mind or heart the more readily by turning 'He scattered his foes' into 'He dissipated his inimical forces,' nor by making 'I have no proud looks' into 'I exhibit no superciliousness.' Nor would an officer gain much good by crying, 'Dextral rotation' for 'Rightwheel.' "[7] His own experience as a country schoolmaster and country preacher convinced him that he knew which kind of language appealed to the common English man. This was the natural, powerful Saxon-English which, through centuries of Latinization, had been preserved by the farmers, the seamen, sailors, and fishermen, and the craftsmen, blacksmiths, and carpenters. In its variety and vigor he saw it as being vastly superior to Latinized standard English.

Barnes's democratic political tendencies, too, seemed to lead him to the position of advocating a national language based on Saxon-English. As a teacher, he knew that one of the manifestations of the differences between an uneducated man and an educated one is vocabulary. Such a language as the one he advocated when used by the entire population would go far in erasing lines drawn between individuals. Since he believed that each man's intrinsic worth was equal to any other man's, the elimination of artificial social barriers between men was highly desirable. The Latinized vocabulary of the educated, Barnes maintained, was hard to understand for the unschooled, and thus drove a wedge between men.

Thence English has become so much harder to learn, that in its foreign-worded fulness, it is a speech only for the more learned and foreign to unschooled men, so that the sermon and the book are half lost to their minds: whereas in Tuscany and in the west of Ireland, or in Wales, the speech of the upper ranks is that of the cottage, and the well-worded book of the higher mind needs no list of hard words to open its meaning to the lower.[8]

Thus, the plain, natural language is serviceable to all, educated and uneducated, teacher and pupil. Barnes put his theory into practice, too, in that visitors to his Sunday services could witness the preacher giving his sermons in a "terse Anglo-Saxon"[9] which was understood by the least-schooled person in the village.

His own Dorset dialect, too, influenced Barnes in the direction of non-Latinized English. Raised with its sounds around him, he knew its strength and efficacy. As he began his study of philology, he saw that Dorset was purer than standard English in that the dialect evolved from its Old English roots, whereas standard English changed by adopting foreign words and forms. The dialect, on the one hand, had preserved the rich stores of words which were present in the old language while the standard language had rejected these in favor of words less familiar, at least to much of the population. Barnes recognized that the Dorset dialect, contrary to popular belief, "is not degraded English but a tongue in its own right which simply developed from the same Anglo-Saxon base. Indeed, had geographical and political factors entered into the formation of our language, we might all be speaking Dorset to-day and calling it English."[10] Barnes saw the Dorset dialect as pure and efficient, while he considered standard English alien and difficult. For him the choice was clear.

Se Gefylsta: An Anglo-Saxon Delectus Serving as a First Class-Book of the Language was published in 1849, demonstrating Barnes's expertise and interest in Old English. The study of Old English is important, he says, because "Anglo Saxon (English) has not been cultivated into a better form, but has been corrupted for the worse, since King Alfred's days."[11] This idea, that modern language is corrupted from an earlier, purer form, is shared by many other linguists in the late eighteenth and early nineteenth centuries.[12] *Se Gefylsta* was written during a period when Barnes was spending his vacation time at Cambridge studying for his degree. Records tell us that the books he took from the university library included many on philology, including grammars of Egyptian, Armenian, Albanian, Chaldean, Anglo-Saxon, and Gothic.[13] His reading material shows how his study of languages was at the same time diffuse and intensive; he tried to make his education as broad as possible and yet as deep as he could dig. *Se Gefylsta,* or *The Helper,* is a case in point. The work is a textbook, and functions well in that capacity by giving an excellent overview of the language. But the grammar is more than a textbook, in that it goes deeply into the theory of language. As Jacobs points out,[14] Barnes here gives the reader a glimpse of an idea which was to become central to his philological thought. This idea is that almost all words have evolved from some basic roots, and while Barnes does not explain the theory in detail here, he does allude to it. In the glossary, Barnes makes the following list:

B*RG, to hide protect
    Burh, (burg) . . . a town, fortified town, fastness, castle. Hence, *borough,* a rabbit's *burrow,* and *burg,* in the name of places.
F*D, this root means "to feed" or "food" thence Fēd-an . . . to feed. Thence "fat," as if "fed," and "father" as if "feeder."
Fōda . . . food
Foster (as if fōdster, a feeder)[15]

The asterisk denotes the position of the vowel, substitution of the vowel being one of the ways in which words change and evolve from the roots. Later, in his 1862 volume entitled *Tiw,* Barnes develops this theory more fully.

The example from the glossary shows the philologist's penchant for etymologizing, a contagious habit for language scholars of this time. Like Tooke's, Barnes's etymologies were sometimes based on a false judgment, and one wrong turn on these trails can lead into some strange territory indeed. His ideas on "fat" and "father" in the example are samples of this misdirection. Given the theory, though—that all words are evolved from certain roots—etymology is a necessary part of the proof, and in fairness to Barnes it should be said that much of his work done tracing the derivations of words turned out to be correct even in the light of more modern linguistics.

In addition to the root word theory, another set of ideas lies beneath the surface of Barnes's Old English grammar. He sees Anglo-Saxon English as being purer than the modern because the newer tongue has lost many of its inflections and, more important, because the modern has allowed many useful, descriptive native words—"good" words, as Barnes says—to be displaced by foreign forms which are less clear. This loss of purity is destructive because Anglo-Saxon, like German, holds within itself the elements of utmost richness. The language's ability to unite words readily into compounds, for instance, provides a gold mine of linguistic adaptability and response. But the constant displacement of Anglo-Saxon words by those of Greek or Latin derivation destroys this kind of ability, thus depriving English speakers of much more than just the words themselves.

The Philological Grammar

Much of Barnes's early philological thoughts and studies came together in a major work, *A Philological Grammar*. Published in 1854, the book is designed as a universal grammar for all languages; it purports to set down the fundamental principles of language which can be applied to any and all tongues. *A Philological Grammar*, like most great works, evolved over a period of years. When he was studying languages at Mere, Barnes discovered that the same laws of case applied to each of the fourteen languages he had worked with up until that time. This discovery was reported in an article, "On the Laws of Case," which was published in the May 1841 number of *Gentlemen's Magazine*. Later, he amplified his views in a small book, *Investigations of the Laws of Case in Language*, published in 1841. This work contained the seed for the *Philological Grammar* in that it expounds on the idea of universal grammar although it was based on the study of only the fourteen languages. In addition, *Investigations of the Laws of Case in Language* provides most of the material for the section in the larger work on the case of nouns.

His studies at Cambridge during periods of 1847 through 1850 provided him with more extensive evidence. He was able to see that his laws applied not only to the fourteen languages studied earlier, but to many others as well. As his work deepened and widened, he was soon able to begin the study of a new language and, within two weeks, to read and write with only the aid of a dictionary. This was done by applying those principles which he saw to remain the same in all tongues. As time went on, he became surer of his universal principles. *A Philological Grammar* is his attempt to bring forth those principles. In his preface, he says,

There are three sciences which are of great service for the strengthening of the mind and the sharpening of wit, and for the helping of the understanding in its search after truth—Geometry, Logic, and Grammar; but if we would make Grammar truly worthy of its two fellow sciences, we must seek to conform it to the universal or to some common laws of speech, so as to make it the science of the language of mankind, rather than the grammar of one tongue.

A knowledge of the forms which have grown out of common laws, working with peculiar elements in one tongue, cannot be fairly taken for the science of Grammar, any more than a knowledge of the organs of one plant (when some even of them are misformed from accidental causes) is the science of Botany.

The formation of language is always a conformation of three things in nature—(1) the beings, actions, and relations of things in the universe; (2) the conceptions of them by the mind of man; and (3) the actions of the organs of speech: and inasmuch as the beings, actions, and relations of things and the mind and the organs of speech are the same in kind to all men upon earth, and a need of conformity to them is itself a law, so far it is clear that some common laws must hold in the formation of languages; and the science of those laws, when they are unfolded, is Grammar.[16]

Having stated his principles, Barnes goes on to say that he is in complete agreement with Pablo Pedrode Astarloa y Aguilla, the author of *Apologia de la Lengua Basconcada,* or *Apology for the Basque Language,* when he says, "A blind slaver to the Greek and Latin languages, and a readiness to believe that every thing which imitates their idioms must be so far regular, has misdirected or fettered our whole literature" (*PG,* v–vi). Barnes adds that he has grounded his work upon English and that the book will serve as an English grammar as well as a universal one. He goes on to list the more than sixty languages from which he drew his principles and forms.

After humbly offering this list, Barnes gives some introductory definitions, first describing grammar as the science of speech and

then speech as the formation and utterance of "breathsounds" by
which men communicate thoughts. He divides his breathsounds
into pure and clipped, or articulate, ones. These breathsounds are
formed by streams of breath which are acted upon by the organs of
speech, namely, the throat, tongue, lips, palate, teeth, and nostrils.
A pure breathsound is one which begins and ends with a stream of
breath flowing through the throat and mouth without any motion
of the other speech organs. It is formed by the speaker setting his
throat and mouth in the one position in which he can begin and
end the sound again and again without altering it with the action
of lips, teeth, or other organs. Examples are the sounds of long *o*
or *e*. A clipped or articulate breathsound, on the other hand, is one
which depends on the action or movement of the organs of speech
for its sound. *Do, to,* and *pat* are examples of breathsounds which
are clipped. So clipped breathsounds are made up of pure breathsounds incorporated with the motions of the organs of speech. Barnes
adds that all breathsounds are either short or long: a short one takes
up only "the least length of time in which a single clipped breathsound can be uttered; as in *bat, met,* and *not*"; a long one "takes up
twice the time of the short one; as in *bate, meet,* and *not*" (*PG*, 2).

While single breathsounds are called syllables, Barnes says, one
or more syllables can make up words. Words are defined as tokens
or symbols of "notions, as man, horseman, white, skilful, walk,
ride; or of relations, as fast, slow, over, under."

Words, composed of breathsounds, make up language which, in
its most natural form, acts on the sense of hearing. But most people,
Barnes notes, have a need for language which can be perceived by
senses other than hearing, since sound is confined to a small sphere
of space around the speaker and is limited to the time in which it
is uttered. So men have developed types or visible marks by which
breathsounds, thus words, and therefore thoughts, can be com-
municated through sight.

The two modes of communicating the words of language by visible
marks are the alphabetic or phonographic mode and the symbolic
or logographic mode. The first symbolizes pure or clipped breathsounds by means of marks called letters; the second symbolizes entire
words with its own mark. Examples of the alphabetic mode are
English and Greek, while an example of the symbolic mode is
Chinese. Language which is characterized by the substitution of
visible marks for the words or syllables Barnes calls "type-language."

Type-language, Barnes says, has been of great help to mankind morally, intellectually or educationally, and socially. Men are able to speak to other men who live generations later by means of type-language; learning and knowledge, arts and science have been passed down through the centuries by type-language.

Other modes of conveying ideas are signals and tokens. Examples of signals are the ringing of bells to announce dinner, the clapping of hands to denote approval, and the blowing of trumpets to call soldiers to specific duties. As examples of tokens, he gives coats of arms to denote family, rings to show marriage, and military badges to demonstrate rank. While these signals and tokens act in such a way as to convey meaning, Barnes says that such systems cannot be called true language. The reason for this is that they are not breathsounds nor are they visible marks of breathsounds.

Having thus introduced his reader to language in general, Barnes turns to some particulars. Type-language, he says, is broken down into four divisions: orthography, etymology, syntax, and prosody. Breathsound language does not deal with orthography, of course, but since the grammar is produced in type-language, the author goes on to discuss it. The four type-language divisions, along with a fifth, rhyme, comprise the main sections of the grammar.

Barnes's orthography is rather conventional; it is his explanations of why words are spelled as they are and his adherence to a program which would introduce a phonotypic alphabet on a national scale which make his orthography noteworthy. Some of his spelling terminology is unfamiliar since it must be compatible with the rest of his theory—for instance, vowels are the letters that spell the pure breathsounds, according to Barnes, while consonants are letters that spell the motions of the organs of speech in the clipped breathsounds—but most of it is in line with common practice.

In his discussion of clippings—the sound which occurs when the motion of the speech organs act upon a stream of air, or consonant sound—Barnes gets at the reason for the existence of unpronounced letters in many spellings of English words. This occurs most often in words that are "worn"; the letter of the clipping stays in the type language although it does not stand for anything in the breathsound speech. He gives many examples of English words in which this occurs: "gnash," "high," "walk," "autumn," "subtle," "comb," and so on. There are several reasons for the occurrence of these silent letters, the first being that old, worn words in a language often succumb to a tendency to replace sounds which are hard to pronounce with ones which are easier. Second, many words are imported into a language along with their original spellings; since the same letter in different languages may represent a different sound, spelling anomalies in borrowed words are common. Moreover, as Barnes correctly points out, letters very often spell more than one sound. Hard and soft *c* and *g* and the variant sounds of *th* are good examples of sounds and their letters that can often become troublesome. This is related to Barnes's final point on the subject which is that each sound in a language does not have a corresponding, unique letter. We have, by his count, sixteen pure breathsounds, or vowels, but only seven letters—*a, e, i, o, u, w, y*—to write them. On the other hand, we have sixteen pure clipping sounds, but nineteen letters to represent them—Barnes sees *c, q,* and *x* as being forms of other consonants. Thus, the type-language does not correspond to the breathsound speech, and this results in a puzzling and difficult state of affairs. But, according to Barnes, this situation need not continue:

This untruthfulness of our spelling is a great hindrance and evil to our children and others in their learning of our type language, and some English grammarians have sought to reduce it according with our breathsound-speech. The best method to this end seems to be that of the upfilling of our alphabet by new letters—formed, as far as possible from the elementary strokes of those we have—for the breath sounds and clipping which are not now marked by letters of their own, and by throwing aside all but one of those that now stand for the same clipping or breath sound.

Such an alphabet has been formed and published by Messrs. PITMAN. It is called the Phonotypic or Phonographic Alphabet, and contains letters not only for most of the voice-sounds and articulations, but also for the diphthongs. (*PG,* 20)

Barnes goes on to advocate the adoption of such a system and to anticipate the opposition's arguments. As a linguistic preservation-ist, even reactionary, he takes care to speak to the issue concerning contemporary standard spelling as a brake on the corruption of language. While he sees this function as a good one, he goes on to say, "The conservative nature of type language is good as long as it can conserve the breathsound speech; but when, notwithstanding the backholding nature of type-language, words have already worn off wholly and for ever from old forms, its conservative power, as to those words, is no longer of any good, and all recommendations

of it, grounded upon the good of its conservative nature, are idle"
(*PG*, 22). Change is inevitable, he says, and the type-form of the
language must follow the immutations of the breathsound language;
otherwise, the type-form in time loses its reason for being.

The section on orthography thus closes with a plea for the adoption
of a system of phonetic spelling. In this, Barnes was in the middle
of a lively nineteenth-century controversy. This issue was debated
at the meetings of the Philological Society of London, in the newspapers, and even in Parliament. Obviously, the forces of reform
lost, but the issue stimulated the concoction of several systems
ranging from the sensible to the crackpot. Sir Isaac Pitman's approach, it should be pointed out, was one of the more moderate
programs. Pitman and A. J. Ellis, along with Barnes and others
were at the forefront of alphabetic reform. Work by a number of
scholars resulted in C. R. Lepsius's *Standard Alphabet* (1855). This
led to Henry Sweet's broad romic system and later, in 1899, to the
revised International Phonetic Alphabet. So while a phonetic alphabet never caught on popularly, the interest in such systems led
to the cooperative development and international codification of this
important linguistic tool.

Fully one half of *A Philological Grammar* deals with etymology,
a subject which Barnes defines as the science of the formation of
different kinds of words. He says, "thoughts are thoughts of things,
with their qualities and beings, and actions, and relations; and words
are of different kinds, as tokens of qualities and beings, and actions
and relations of things" (*PG*, 28). Most grammarians, Barnes says,
recognize nouns, pronouns, adjectives, verbs, adverbs, prepositions,
and interjections; he sees all words as being either notional or relational. Notional words—nouns, adjectives, and verbs—stand for
ideas of being or action. Relational words, on the other hand, are
tokens of the relations of things. These include pronouns, adverbs,
and prepositions. Notional words, like "man" or "good," are called
root-words, while others, like "manly" and "goodness," are called
derivative words. The relational words are always formed from roots
and thus are always derivational.

Barnes explains the process by which the sounds of words—and
therefore languages—evolve and change. There is a tendency in all
languages to make clipping breathsounds, sounds indicated by consonants, smoother and easier rather than rougher and harder. Further, some languages show a disposition to some kinds of sounds

rather than some others; when a word introduced to a language contains a sound that the language is not disposed toward, that sound is often changed to a more compatible one or simply left out. So changes occur in the "wearing" of a word, in which a difficult to pronounce sound is gradually replaced by one which is less harsh, and in the importing of a foreign word, in which a less compatible sound is replaced by a more acceptable one or is eliminated altogether. Barnes goes on to give examples of changes of this kind which have taken place; he also sets down the principles according to which such changes are made, the principles having been formed from his observations of the sixty-odd languages. The work done here is a continuation and extension of Grimm's earlier work on consonant change in the Indo-European group.

The process of word derivation or evolution from roots employs these rules of sound change, but it follows other principles as well. Barnes says that all man's notions are ones of either action or existence, ideas of action being a necessary precondition of ideas of existence. Thus, root verbs—which stand for or "betoken" ideas of action—are necessary to the formation of words denoting ideas of existence. Roots, the words from which all others are derived, are verbs. Examples of noun stems derived from verb roots are "chip" from "chop," "hinge" from "hang," "hilt" from "hold," "song" from "sing," and "tale" from "tell." Barnes goes on to say that notions of the activities of the mind or of things which are not perceived by the senses—abstract ideas—are mostly formed from notions of the activities of the body or of things perceived by the senses. Two examples of this are the derivation of the French *penser*— "to think," or "to weigh in the mind"—from the Latin *pendo*—"to weigh"—and the formation of the German *begreifen*—"to comprehend"—from *greif-en*—"to lay hold of." Compounding is another method of word formation. This process involves the linking of words as in the putting together of two nouns to form "railway," of an adjective and a noun to form "blackbird," or of a preposition and a verb to form "overcome." The five types of words which can be used in this process are nouns, verbs, prepositions, adjectives, and adverbs. Barnes lists several examples in which words are formed to denote particular functions, such as nouns of place and nouns of quality, and he shows how changes in number and gender are indicated by his principles.

In his section on etymology, Barnes includes a good deal of material on the case of nouns, a subject which had interested him from his earliest linguistic studies. He reviews theories of case as put forth by twelve grammarians in several languages, demonstrating the lack of agreement on this subject among these scholars. His argument for the cases of nouns, a principle which applies to all languages, lists twelve cases: nominative, vocative, possessive, genitive or elative, originative, accusative or illative, allitive or objective, locative, dative or adessive, associative or instrumentive, abessive, and assecutive. Not willing to leave well enough alone, Barnes proceeds to a discussion of what he calls twofold cases. These he defines as ambiguous cases in which "It may so happen that, notwithstanding the clear off-taking of one case of another, the relation of a thing (A) to another (B) may be such, that (A) may be fairly taken as in either of two logical relations to (B); and therefore that one case may be taken in language for another" (*PG,* 121–22). In his discussion of case, Barnes has insisted that case denotes the relationship of things to one another and not the relationship of words to one another, so instead of having to account only for the workings of language, he gets into a much larger realm. Lest the reader shrink at the task, the indomitable Dorsetman says,

It may be said against a system of natural cases, [that is, cases of actual things rather than of words] that to discriminate so many classes of the logical relations of things upon what may be deemed slight differences of likenesses, and to unfold so many shiftings of twofold cases [fifty-six examples], is to make grammar needlessly perplexing. To this it may be answered, that all the logical relations of *things* [my italics] are in nature, and if they are manifold there is no help for it: we may shut our eyes to them, but we cannot lessen them. They have been brought in sundry classes under the thought of men of all nations, as they have shown by the structure of their languages, and our minds will miss the good of what should be a wit-sharpening exercise, the learning of grammar, if we wilfully keep them out of thought. (*PG,* 144–45)

Barnes's learned but cumbersome case system does reduce the study of grammar to an exercise; as to whether or not it is wit-sharpening, only the individual reader can judge. This formulation is unusable for all practical purposes, yet fortunately it does not mar the other contributions of the volume; the system is a demonstration of Barnes's meticulous regard for thoroughness and an indication of the original thinking that went into this work.

The rest of the section on etymology is mostly orthodox, although Barnes's system of word formation is in evidence throughout. He shows how derivative words formed from roots by means of compounding or through consonant or vowel changing. His examples in English are always supplemented with examples from foreign languages; while he intends for his book to be used primarily as an English grammar, he wishes for it to be apparent that his ideas are based on principles which apply to all languages.

In the section entitled "Syntax," Barnes discusses standard usage and sentence structure, setting out a number of rules on these topics. Again, this is orthodox fare, until the end of the chapter where are found appended two short essays, "Purity" and "Ethnology and Language." In the first, he says,

> A language is called purer inasmuch as more of its words are formed from its own roots.
> Purity is deemed a good quality of languages, inasmuch as the purer a language is, the more regular it is in clippings and breath-sounds, and in the forms of its words and sentences; and the more readily it is learnt and understood. (*PG,* 258)

A plea follows for the purification of English in which he exhorts the reader to cast off words of Latin and Greek derivation and turn to the Old English roots. Throw off "exaggerate," he says, and take up "greaten"; use "fore-draught" for "program," "bendsome" for flexible. He praises a writer in a magazine for using "undersea" instead of "submarine," and goes so far as to translate a New Testament passage from Latin-rooted to English words.

In "Ethnology and Language," he discusses how nations are grouped, or "off-marked" into races which come from a common stock, and how they speak languages which come from the same roots and have the same structure. As a "law of languages," he states the principle that when nations or tribes mingle through warfare or the appropriation of land, the language of the incoming race will be grafted onto that of the overcome nation. The incoming language will not replace the other, however, until the number of newcomers surpasses the number of natives; the fewer yield their language to the greater number. This accounts, he says, for the fact that the language of the Teutonic Angles and Saxons dominated that of the Celtic Britons and for other linguistic changes as well.

The last two sections of *A Philological Grammar* are concerned with prosody and rhyme, taking into account Hebrew, Persian, and Welsh poetry, as well as that of English and the better-known languages. Again, Barnes embellishes his assertions with copious examples, demonstrating not only knowledge of other languages and literatures, but command of them.

Although *A Philological Grammar* affirms his belief in a "pure" English based on Saxon-English by advocating an eradication of Latinate forms and their replacement by Teutonic root derivatives, Barnes's own practice in writing the book falls short of his goal. An examination of his vocabulary shows that he does make an attempt to introduce Saxon words and terms to some extent; his use of "breathing" and "clipping" for "vowel" and "consonant" are good examples. Yet this is not done with any programmatic thoroughness. Technical terms like "prothesis," "epenthesis," and "paragoge" are retained in their classical forms as are rhetorical terms like "diaresis," "iambus," "dactyl," and "amphibrach." The diction overall is a blend of Saxon and Latinate in just such a ratio that we can sense the beginnings of the heavily Saxon style that Barnes was to use later.

A Philological Grammar achieved two of Barnes's primary ends. First, it provided an English grammar constructed according to what Barnes saw as a set of principles universal to all languages. In this, the work succeeds, describing the language according to both original and accepted linguistic theories. Second, it presented a rationale and plan of action for the replacement of imported, foreign words by pure English ones. While the work was a formidable achievement from several points of view, Barnes did not end his philological scholarship with its publication.

Tiw, the Hopeful Brat

Tiw, published in 1862, was a continuation of one aspect of his work in *A Philological Grammar.* Its subtitle, *A View of the Roots and Stems of the English as a Teutonic Language,* is a fair description of what Barnes liked to call his "hopeful brat." The work is an attempt to trace English, and indeed, the other Germanic languages back to their origin, Tiw being the name of the god from whom the

Teutonic race took its name. The work succeeds in its intention, in that it is a very thorough examination and explanation of the process of language evolution. While he deals only with the Germanic family here, he believed that all languages might eventually be traced back to the same set of roots.

My view of the English, as a Teutonic tongue, is that the bulk of it was formed from about fifty primary roots, of such endings and beginnings as the sundry clippings that are still in use by the English organs of speech. I have reached these roots through the English provincial dialects and other Teutonic speech forms, and I deem them the primary ones, inasmuch as, by the known course of Teutonic word-building and word-wear, our sundry forms of stem-words might have come from them, but could not have yielded them.

He then lists the primary roots, explaining that the star indicates the place of a variable voicing, or vowel sound. Barnes recommends that the reader use an *i* sound when pronouncing the root, since that one is most common in Teutonic languages. Examples are *cr*ng, fl*ng, d*ng,* and *pl*ng.*

Barnes saw the natural process of word-wear working on these roots, changing the *ng* endings to *nk,* as *cr*ng* to *crank;* or *ng* to *nge,* as *cr*ng* to "cringe" or *ng* to *nch,* as *fl*ng* to "flinch"; or *ng* to *g,* as *d*ng* to "dig"; or *ng* to *dge,* as *pl*ng* to "pledge." Other variations of *ng* formed by speech-wear Barnes lists as *k, tch,* and the dropping of *ng* altogether. As long as root-words wear from *ng* to one of these other nine endings, Barnes continues to call them roots. When, however, the endings change to another kind, he refers to them as stems.

He sets up a number of tables in which he shows how certain endings combine with roots to form stems. For example, *F*ng* might take the *st* ending to form the stem "fast," *Spl*ng* could take the *sk, sh* ending to become "splash," or *Pr*ng* might take the *b, p,* and *f* ending to form "prop."

In addition to the change of endings, other mutations are possible in the Teutonic tongues as well. Substitutions in vowel sounds contribute to the word-building process, as in the change from "steep" to "step," "melt" to "molt," or "smell" to "small." The initial sound, too, might change to form a completely new word: "bear" to "tear," for example, or "sprawl" to "crawl" or "drawl." The list of possible variations of the forty-nine basic roots, using only initial, ending, and vowel change, is very large indeed. Add the process of compounding words—uniting nouns, verbs, adjectives, adverbs, and propositions—and the supply is virtually endless.

While Barnes says that his view of the English roots has not yet taken in all English words—prepositions, pronouns, and others still have to be examined—he maintains that his theory is valuable for several reasons. First, from this idea it can be seen that the provincial dialects are not jargons or corruptions of the "standard" language, but "true and good forms of Teutonic speech." Second, a knowledge of stem-building from primary roots should lead us to a more accurate use of words and better definitions in our dictionaries. Too, the process should lead us to a better understanding of the relationships between words. Finally, Barnes says, the theory demonstrates the relationships between languages. If two languages have evolved from the same set of roots, it stands to reason that many words in both will be similar or alike. In this regard, he warns against "taking sisterhood for motherhood in speech; so that when we find an English word in the same or like form in Gothic, or German, or Latin, or Greek, we may at once think that the English had it from the other language, to which we may thus impute the motherhood of it. Whereas both languages, as sisters, may have it now from the now lost mother-speech."[17] Barnes, like many of the other nineteenth-century philologists, was speculating on the *Ursprache.*

After explaining the theory and its basis, Barnes presents his evidence. Beginning with *B*ng,* he goes through his list of root-words, offers a general definition of the meaning of the root, and then gives examples of modern words which have evolved from the root. For example, he takes *B*ng* as

1. To be or to set up, bear up, or make up together, as in a store, in a bunch or mass, in a building.
   From the primary meaning it takes that of to bend up; and
2. To bend all round, to inclose.
3. To beat with something bunch-like, unless it is another form of the root P*ng.
4. To make sounds the type of which was that of a hollow body.

Examples he gives are "bung," "bank," "bang," "bunker," "bunch," and many others. This procedure is followed until the forty-nine roots are accounted for; the result is an impressive demonstration of philological erudition, with Barnes supplying obsolete and obsolescent words and definitions in a manner which would make the editors of the *Oxford English Dictionary* envious. He uses many dialect and Old English words and terms not as historical oddities, but because of his belief that they are valuable and should be rejuvenated as integral parts of the language. Some examples are *briggan*, "to build"; *feck*, "handsomeness"; *nesh*, "bedsome," "soft and yielding"; and *wanluck*, "ill luck". Some of Barnes's etymological work is accurate, while some is not. The extent of his accuracy is surprising, though, in light of his relative lack of reliable source materials.

The style of *Tiw* is more Saxonized than is *A Philological Grammar*, but surprisingly, the result is not stiff or artificial. Barnes deftly avoids Latinate words and substitutes instead words standard to the language but derived from the Old English. It is evident that as time went on, Barnes was practicing what he preached and in the process proving that what he advocated was possible.

Yet Barnes's Saxon style was not admired by all. In offering the support of the Philological Society for Barnes's *A Grammar and Glossary of the Dorset Dialect*, F. J. Furnivall added a stipulation, demanding that Barnes "substitute the usual terms for the unusual ones—as voice (sounds), voicings (vowels), clippings for consonants, mate-words for synonyms, etc., there being no reason to introduce such quaint and unhappy words—what notion does clippings convey to one's mind?—especially as other terms—diphthongs, pronouns, etc., are retained and 'vowels' is used more than once."[18] To the surprise of many, Barnes agreed, and the work was published in 1863.

Dorset Grammar and Glossary

The Dorset Grammar and Glossary deals with two central issues: first, it discusses the nature of the dialect, and second, it makes several useful applications of Dorset to English. In his remarks on the dialect itself, Barnes asserts that Dorset is a language rather than a corruption of standard English. To many philologists in the nineteenth century, dialects were taken to be speech patterns based on the conventional language of a nation, but distorted by uneducated people. Dorset was thus seen by many as being a rustic misapplication of the language spoken in London; Barnes presumed to set the record straight. He shows that the dialect developed independently of the standard language, in the process retaining many of the older, purer forms: "The old speech of the land-folk of the south-west of England, seems to have come down, with a variation hardly quicker than that of the usual offwearing of speech-forms, from the language which our foreelders, the followers of the Saxon leaders Cordic and Cynric, Porta, Stuf, and Wihtgar, brought from the south of Denmark, their inland seat."[19]

The reader can see from his use of words like "foreelders," "land-folk," and "offwearing" that Furnivall did not entirely discourage Barnes's determination to use the non-Latinate forms. Barnes goes on to say that not only did Dorset develop independently from English, but that it retained many of the old words and old methods of word-formation that the standard tongue had done away with. The Dorset habit of compounding of prefixes like "for" and suffixes like "some" Barnes sees as a valuable process in increasing a language's word store, but this custom has largely passed out of use in English. The vocabulary of Dorset, too, he sees as retaining a Teutonic flavor, while English has long since turned its back on its Germanic background and embraced Latin as a supplier of new words. This tendency on the part of English he sees as being needless and wasteful:

In searching the word-stores of the provincial speech-forms of English, we cannot but behold what a wealth of stems we have overlooked at home, while we have drawn needful supplies of words from other tongues; and how deficient is even English itself without the synonyms which our land-folk are ready to give it, and how many old root and stem forms of words are used by people who might be thought to have corrupted even later forms of them.[20]

Learn from the dialects, Barnes urged. English could become both simpler and richer by following the dialects, purging the language of its Latinate forms, and embracing words of Germanic extraction.

Outline of English Speechcraft

In 1878, Barnes brought out *An Outline of English Speechcraft,* the culmination of all his philological efforts. The author clearly states his purpose in his "Fore-say" when he says that his effort is "one small trial, weak though it may be, towards the upholding of our own strong old Anglo-Saxon speech, and the ready teaching of it to purely English minds by their own tongue."[21]

Most admirable in Barnes is his habit of using his knowledge to teach others; he is not an idealistic romantic searching for a far-off blazing star of truth, nor does he seek knowledge for its own sake. For Barnes, the roles of scholar and teacher intertwine, and learning by itself has little value unless it can be passed on to others and put to good use. His practice of writing and preaching in Saxon English is a case in point: while it was important for him to do this in order to demonstrate that his ideas on linguistic purism are practical, his main purpose, he says, is pedagogical:

I have tried to teach English by English, and so have given English words for most of the lore-words [scientific terms], as I believe they would be more readily and more clearly understood, and, since we can better keep in mind what we do than what we do not understand, they would be better remembered. There is, in the learning of that charmingly simple and yet clear speech, pure Persian, now much mingled with Arabic, a saddening check; for us sooner does a learner come to the time-words than he is told that he should learn, what is then put before him, an outline of Arabic Grammar. And there are tokens that, ere long the English youth will want an outline of the Greek and Latin tongues ere he can well understand his own speech. (O, iv)

And teach English by English he does, but it is the English of Germanic roots he uses rather than the Latinate version used in "cultivated" society. "If a man should walk with me through our village, I could show him many things of which we want to speak every day, and for which we have words of which Johnson knew nothing" (O, v).

His diction suits his purpose and his audience well, for his language fits his purist theory, thus appealing to the philologically sophisticated; yet his words are understood by the least educated of his readers, those for whom he intended this work as a first English grammar. He anticipates the arguments of critics who might contend that a grammar should put forth linguistic principles embraced by the cultured elite rather than the common rustic. In his thoroughly modern belief that a grammar should be descriptive, rather than prescriptive, Barnes says, "If a man would write a grammar of a speech, of which there is yet none, what could he do but show it forth as it is in the shape which its best speakers over the land hold to be its best? To hold that a tongue had no shape, or a bad one, ere a grammar of it was written, seems much like saying that a man had no face, or a bad one, till his likeness was taken" (*O, vi*).

In his "Heads of Matter," we are first introduced to the terminology Barnes uses for the traditional linguistic nomenclature; a partial listing of his table of contents follows, along with the standard terminology in parentheses: free breathings (vowels); breath-pennings (consonants); thing-names (nouns); outshowing mark words (demonstrative pronouns); suchness (adjectives); time-taking and time-words (verbs); helping time-words (auxiliary verbs); way-marks and stead-marks (prepositions); speech-trimming (diction).

The work may be said to be divided into two parts: the first, "Speech-craft," a descriptive grammar of the English language, complete with Saxonized terms; second, a section entitled "Words of Speech-Craft, and Others, Englished," which is a selective glossary of Latinate English words with Saxon synonyms and a conclusion consisting of two essays, "The Power of the Word-endings" and "Goodness of a Speech." Both sections are worth comment.

In the first part Barnes attempts to describe English as he finds it. Words of Anglo-Saxon derivation are used in the descriptions and examples, but he uses comparative grammar wherever it is needed to explain principles. In these latter cases, of course, Barnes uses the language to which English is being compared. An example is his explanation of what he calls "time-name":

A time-taking, taken as a deed or being without any time-taking thing, is taken as a *thing,* and its name is a *thing-name,* as *to write.*
As in Greek the Infinitive mood, *to graphien,* the "to write"; and in Italian, *il scrivere,* the "to write" (the deed of writing or a writing), so the Infinitive mood-shape of the Saxon time-word (verb) was taken as a thing-name (noun) after the preposition *to,* to or for, as *to huntianne* (to or for the deed to hunt or hunting), as 'Why does Alfred keep those dogs?' "To huntianne." (*O,* 16)

Thus Barnes uses the relatively modern technique of comparative grammar to illustrate his points.

He also employs historical linguistics when it is necessary. In the following, he uses an historical approach in his discussion of the use of the present participle form as either a gerund or an adjective:

Unhappily two sundry endings of the old English have worn into one shape. They were -*ung* or -*ing* and -*end*.
Singung is the deed of singing, a thing. *Singend* is a mark-word, as in the wording "I have a singing bird."
Sailing and *hunting*, in the foregiven thought-wordings, are thing-names, and not mark-words. *Sailing* is *segling*, as 'ne mid *segling* ne mid rownesse' (neither with sailing nor rowing). Bede 5, 1.
   "*Wunigende* ofer hyne" (woning [mark-word] over him).—Matt. iii. 16.
   "Sy *wunung* heora on west" (be their *woning* [thing-name] waste).—Ps. lxviii. 30.
   "ne gelaede du us on *costhunge*" (lead us not into *tempting* [thing-name]).—Lord's Prayer. (*O*, 17)

At the end of the section entitled "Speech-Craft," Barnes includes some remarks on speech-trimming, or diction. Here he asserts, as he has so many times, that English words are more clearly understood than those derived from Latin or Greek, and thus misunderstandings can be avoided by embracing the one kind and avoiding the others. He then gives several examples of solecisms, or miswordings as he calls them, which are caused by the use of Latinate words. "One has written 'ideas are manufactured.' By whose hands?" he asks (*O*, 37):

One takes *irretrievable* as nohow amended. If "retrieve" is the French *retrouver* (to find again), "irretrievable" would mean not to be found again; and "the irretrievable defeat of the whole nation" would be one which they could not *find* again, as most likely they would not wish to find it. (*O*, 38)

His discussion at the end of the first part is a fitting introduction to the next section, "Words of Speech-craft, and Others, Englished: With Some Notes." This glossary lists in alphabetical order some three hundred and fifty-odd words of Latin derivation for which definitions are given in Saxon English. Definitions vary in length from the single word to the full page.
   Two essays, "The Power of the Word Endings" and "The Goodness of Speech," conclude the second section. The first makes some

interesting, if unscientific, observations. He begins with the following generalization:

> Some of the small word-endings end themselves with a dead breath-penning [as in the sounds *ak, ap, at, ag, ab, ad*], and the others with a half-penning [the rest of the consonant sounds, for example, *am, av*]. The dead-pennings seem to betoken, mostly an ending, or shortening, or lessening, in time and shape; while the half-pennings do not seem to bound, or shorten, or lessen the meaning of their body-words. (*O, 83*)

He gives copious examples, but the results are inconclusive; sometimes they are purely conjectural: "In the word-ending -*st* of *blackest,* the half-penning *s* freely forstrengthens *black,* and the dead-penning *t* seems to check its force, so that the *blackest* means *black* strengthened, though not unboundedly so, but blackest of all the things taken with it" (*O, 85*). Here, Barnes lapses into unempirical meanderings, reminiscent of some of the worst eighteenth-century philological guesswork. This is hard to account for, since this volume for the most part demonstrates a commitment to the new scientific study of language and even flashes of twentieth-century linguistic techniques.

In his final discussion, "The Goodness of a Speech," Barnes lists the criteria for good language: "clearness to the hearing and mind, clearness of its breathsounds, and clearness in the meaning of its words; in its fulness of words . . . , in sound-sweetness to the ear, and glibness to the tongue" (*O, 86*). *Fulness* he defines as richness of vocabulary, something which English lacks because of the importation of foreign words resulting in the dropping of old words. "Immediately" has replaced "anon," he says, with a corresponding loss of brevity, "ignite" vies with "kindle," "annual" with "yearly," and "machine" with "jinny." The result is that English does not become richer by the addition of foreign words, for the latter tend to force out words of the older language. A good example, Barnes says, are the legal terms which were brought to England by the Norman French and which subsequently thrust aside the old English law-words. *Dema* became "judge"; *borh* became "bail"; *forburning,* "arson"; and *housebreach,* "burglary" with no improvement of the tongue. On the contrary, a whole new set of terms needed to be learned by the conquered natives: "The Latinate and Greekish wording is a hindrance to the teaching of the homely poor, or at least the land folk. It is not clear to them, and some of them say of a clergyman that his Latinised preaching is too high for them and seldom seek the church" (*O*, 88). Thus the Latinate speech, according to Barnes, destroys clarity, his first desideratum for good speech.

Sound-sweetness suffers, too, in modern English. In "our true English," he says, we have many hard consonant sounds adjacent to one another, as in "packed," resulting in a word hard to pronounce and unpleasant to the ear. To add to this sorry situation, Barnes continues, we have brought in a host of foreign words with just the same hardness, like "deflect" and "tract." We should, he says, take a lesson from the dialects and from the Celtic and shun such speech.

Barnes ends his book with an index he calls "Clue to Matters Handled," a fitting end to a work which has been called "a key document . . . in the Anglo-Saxon tradition."[22] It is here that Barnes's purist philosophy is best expressed in that his argument against Latinist encroachment is solidified in the best Saxon English. And while the reader is at first repelled by the onslaught of unfamiliar words and words used unfamiliarly, the effect of the prose soon becomes smooth and comfortable. In many ways, the style and diction are the best argument he could make.

Barnes's Linguistic Contributions

Barnes's interest in the study of language began when he was a young man and continued unabated until his death. His philological articles and books were published over a span of fifty years, beginning with *The Etymological Glossary* in 1829 and ending with *An Outline of Speech-craft* in 1878. The impressive fact about his linguistic scholarship, though, is not its duration or the quantity of publication, but rather that Barnes dealt with most of the major philological questions of his time in an age when language study was undergoing enormous change, when the very nature of the discipline itself was being redefined. This feat is compounded by the facts that Barnes was largely self-educated—his work at Cambridge amounted to little more than a couple of semesters of directed reading—and that he lived his entire life in a relatively isolated rural district of England.

In spite of his physical isolation, Barnes participated in the major efforts of nineteenth-century linguistics. He was aware of and considered the major issues and worked to improve the discipline's methodologies. A *Philological Grammar* is his contribution to the development of a universal grammar, or a set of principles which apply to all languages, a task which held the interest of many philologists of the time. His *Tiw* concerns itself with the origin of speech and another topic of contemporary importance, the existence and identification of the *Ursprache*. He held advanced views in dialectology and correctly asserted that dialects were separate linguistic entities and not simply corruptions of the "standard" language. Like the new philologists and modern linguists, he recognized the importance of including descriptive and historical linguistics in his methodology; he viewed language as an organic and historical entity which is in a constant state of change. As much as any of his contemporaries, Barnes saw language as an integral part of man's social and economic life and of his ethnic and cultural history. His work in spelling reform and Saxonization of the language were activities in the mainstream of contemporary philology, too; many members of the Philological Society of London were actively engaged in attempting to change spelling conventions and scholars of the Northern languages and literatures, like Otto Jesperson, shared Barnes's views on English purism. All in all, his accomplishments in philology are amazing, all the more so because they belong to a provincial country preacher.

Barnes's major contribution to the study of philology was his insistence on the importance of the study of Old English and other Germanic tongues as a way of examining modern English. He saw, too, that the older languages were important for their own sakes, that they were distinct historical entities; while they were linked to more modern languages by certain linguistic processes, nevertheless they existed separately and had their own rich literatures. Barnes saw that the study of Old English and other related languages was important from an historical standpoint, as well as from literary and linguistic ones. History has proved Barnes's perception to be correct.

Chapter Four

Social, Economic, and Historical Interests

The Condition of England

While Barnes lived a relatively secluded life in quiet, rural Dorset, he was concerned about the rapid changes affecting the most basic institutions in contemporary English society. Nothing, it seemed, was sacred in the onslaught of progress which made profound alterations in the social, religious, political, and economic life of every British citizen.

The industrial revolution was literally changing the face of the landscape; even in Dorset, events like the coming of the railroad to link Dorchester and London had a profound impact on much of the local life. Thousands of people all across England whose families had lived on the land forever were forced into the cities, often giving up property and profession. The hardships this caused many farmers is traced in some of Barnes's poetry, specifically in his eclogues. The poet saw centuries-old forms of manufacture and occupation give way to the factory system with its crowded, unsafe conditions and its slavery to the clock. Children worked long hours in factories and women crawled on their hands and knees through the narrow tunnels of coal mines. It was perhaps in reaction to these industrial scenes that Barnes presents his starkly contrasting pastoral landscapes. In any case, he was deeply concerned with the changes he saw being brought to England through industrialization.

Ironically, the industrial revolution provided the catalyst for reform as well, often giving a staggering society additional shocks. Labor unions were organized, as were organizations of agricultural workers affected by the introduction of farm machinery. In Dorset, for example, attempts were made to organize farm workers displaced by machines; Barnes was sympathetic to the problem, if not necessarily to the cure. Eventually child labor, agricultural, and factory reform bills were passed by Parliament, but the process was a lengthy one. Reform affected citizens other than workers, too. The industrial revolution and the factory system concentrated much of the nation's wealth—heretofore in the hands of the aristocracy—in the middle class. This group consisted of bankers, merchants, factory owners, mine operators, and transportation magnates.

The advent of farm machinery and advanced agricultural practices had another effect on the rural society—the concentration of land ownership in the hands of fewer persons who acquired increasingly larger holdings. The result was the rise of a middle class of farmers who resembled the factory owners in the cities in that increases in production and of their capital were their primary concerns. This attitude had a devastating effect on the rural poor. Tennyson chronicles the new captain of agriculture in his "Northern Farmer: New Style," while Barnes treats the effect of this social change on the farm worker and his family in the eclogues.

The concentration of populations around the large factories of the industrial cities, caused to some extent by people being forced off the farmlands by the consolidation of small farms and by the use of the new machines, gave rise to slums and all their attendant miseries. The family structure, in many cases, broke down under the pressures of poverty, overcrowding, and exhaustion. Education for children was meager or nonexistent in many mill towns, crime flourished, and alcoholism and prostitution were rampant. The parish church, so often a refuge during times of trouble in the country, was less effective in the crowded cities.

The foundations of religion itself were shaken by several forces. Scientific discoveries, notably in geology and biology, made it difficult for many to continue to believe in religious teachings which had gone unchallenged for centuries. The idea of evolution, popular for many years before Darwin's publications, became the doctrine of generations of religious skeptics. The churches were attacked from within as well by schismatics and reformers. Sect after sect broke off from the main bodies and formed their own denominations. It was difficult to know just what to believe. In many ways, the time in which William Barnes wrote can best be characterized as an age in search of faith.

One of the manifestations of this quest for faith was an avid interest in history, not only the political history of wars and the succession of kings, but the cultural histories of peoples and races. In many ways, nineteenth-century England was looking for its roots in the hope that these would furnish them with a sense of heritage and direction in a time of change and uncertainty.

Although he lived far from the slums of Manchester and Sheffield, Barnes was attuned to the predicaments of his countrymen. The plight of the agricultural worker, especially, was of immediate concern; he was faced daily with the sight of families forced off their land by the enclosure acts and of farm hands thrown out of work by the adoption of machinery. In addition, in spite of his geographic isolation, Barnes was aware of the great social, economic, and political questions of the day. Characteristically, the man studied these issues, formulated his propositions, and published his findings.

Similarly, he believed that it was important for his countrymen to know all they could about their past, especially about that area of the past which had been largely neglected in the schools. While many school children were steeped in the lore of the Peloponnesian War and the Punic encounters of Rome with Carthage, they knew little or nothing of the clashes of the Celts and the Picts or of the Saxon and Danish invasions of their own island. Barnes knew that to ignore this part of history was for most Britons to remain ignorant about the origins of their own culture, to turn their backs on their racial and linguistic identities. He knew, too, that to ignore the Middle Ages and earlier history was to leave unfinished the portrait of the British nation; for the characteristically thorough and meticulous Dorsetman, this was unspeakable. Typically, Barnes first educated himself in these matters and then set out to educate others.

Social and Economic Views

Views of Labour and Gold presents much of Barnes's social and economic theory. Published in 1859, it also gives many of his views on the condition of England question, an issue which prompted much debate throughout the nineteenth century. The volume, which was originally a compilation of notes for a course of lectures, is organized into a series of essays. Although the essays at first are almost entirely on the subject of economics, they soon branch out into several other areas including religious and social commentary. The main thrust of the remarks does deal, however, with labor and the fruits of labor.

Labour and Gold is the central direct assertion of Barnes's social and economic views. He demonstrates his belief that labor is the basis for wealth and, indeed, for man's well-being. He is not in agreement with contemporary trends, such as the migration from the countryside to the cities, or with contemporary systems and policies, such as the factory system with its reliance on machinery and the division of labor, the concentration of the ownership of land and capital to a relative few, and the national policy toward the poor. In many ways, his social and economic views are preservationist and even reactionary; he would retain what remained of the old ways and values and, if given a choice, probably would turn back the hands of the clock to a pre—industrial revolution England. He looked back to a time when England was chiefly agricultural, when people worked and were rewarded for it fairly, and when each person knew what was expected to achieve success on this earth. Whether or not such a golden age actually existed is not as important as the fact that many thinkers in the nineteenth century—Barnes especially—sought direction for the future from the past.

But in many other ways, though, Barnes anticipated some twentieth-century ideas and attitudes. His warnings against the psychological and spiritual effects on workers of the factory system are ahead of his time. His discussion of the distinction between lawful and circumstantial freedom, too, takes up an important issue in democratic political theory. In general, his views strike a sensible balance between the preservation of time-tested values and the acceptance of well-conceived proposals for change.

In one chapter, "Labour, Gold, and Civilization," he comments on the effects of civilization upon the way in which people earn their livings. At first, in that form we call the savage state, man's labor consisted of meeting his immediate needs; he did this by hunting, fishing, gathering wild foods, and making clothing and shelter for himself. The effect of this labor was twofold: first, it provided man with the wherewithal to go on living, and second, it helped him to develop his physical and mental faculties through the demands such a life placed on him. His muscles were brought into action by the running, crouching, and climbing of the hunt, and his senses were sharpened by the stealth needed in the pursuit.

With the advent of agriculture, though, a change in the social system is introduced. "Civilization has a tendency to divide labour, and give to each man work of one particular kind, and thus to make for him a hand and mind of only one skill."[1] A person ceases to be skillful at all the activities necessary to make his living, and becomes

expert at only one, or a few. While this situation promotes efficiency,
its effects are not entirely good. "Indeed, I believe that excessive
division of labour is most pernicious to the workman's health; for
examples we need only to look to the miner in Cornwall, or to
workers in the glass-blowing industry, or to the man who grinds
needles all day and inhales the steel dust into his lungs" (V, 3).
But the division of labor has another pernicious effect, the loss of
valuable skills. Witness the young women who work in the textile
mills, he says. Formerly they were taught to spin, weave, knit,
quilt, cook, and make cheese, but now all they know is how to
tend a power loom. In the modern world, too, it is possible to be
left completely destitute, without even one's own hands for resources. Barnes says, "An Iceland farmer may be his own timber
and iron worker, and may make his own implements, and build his
own house, and weave his own wadmel [wool cloth], and therefore,
may hang less helplessly on others; but an Englishman, with only
capital, without hand skill, if he loses his capital, which works for
him, may have left a pair of hands unskilled, and so quite insufficient
for his livelihood" (V, 4). The division of labor, then, is not an
unqualified success.

Barnes defines capital as accumulated but transferable labor, or
"work-store." A man may store up capital by working more than
is needed for his own sustenance, or "life-gear." This surplus labor
or life-gear he may save for a rainy day, he may lend, he may give
away to someone in need, or he may squander. Since, however, the
days in which we all produce our life-gear—food, clothing, shelter—have been replaced by the age of the division of labor, systems
of barter and money have come to be needed. The farmer will trade
some of his grain for a few of the fisherman's fish, the weaver will
barter his cloth for the dairyman's cheese. Such dealings in life-
gear, or commodities, have gone on for centuries and still go on in
certain parts of society. But complications arose with this system,
too; a man or a tribe might need some commodity from a store of
another person or group who might not want his. Further, many
commodities are perishable and thus are not suited to be stored for
future use. The result is that money was invented. While this was
probably necessary, Barnes says, it is not entirely auspicious; money's
very convenience encourages stealing and hoarding.

After a chapter in which he discusses the history of coins, the
author takes up capital's relationship to bullion, and then to wealth

and interest. As to the first, he says, "Bullion should not be mistaken for capital. Capital and bullion are different things, as one of them may increase while the other is constant. The bullion of a people is the weight of the money or money-metals in their hands; and the capital of a people is their quantity of stored labour, or of their labour on hand in any form, or in all forms of life-gear." He goes on to point out that "without labor there is no increase of capital" (*V*, 17).

Barnes makes a distinction between capital and wealth by pointing out that wealth is accumulated life-gear or commodities or else possessions of value like unworked mines or waters full of fish. Capital, on the other hand, is only the wealth of labor. Interest he defines as the rent of capital; its rate fluctuation is due to the availability of capital and to the reputation of the borrower, hard facts then as now.

Barnes next turns to the determination of value, distinguishing between the real value and the commercial value of a product or service. These may be the same, but more often they vary. For instance, the real value—or life-worth—of air is so great that we cannot live without it. On the other hand, air is in such abundance that its commercial value—or money-worth—is nothing. Too, the commercial value of one thing may exceed that of another, even though the real value is obviously less. For example, iron is of more real value than gold, yet there is a wide disparity in the commercial value of each. "Money is a form of stored labours, and is of no good where there is no labour-won life-gear, or where there is a fulness of freely given life-gear" (*V*, 26). Money is of little use to a starving man if there is no food to buy. Barnes's advice in such a world is that of Queen Elizabeth: "Take to sea such goods as you can carry off in a wreck; or get such goods as you can take on with you if your fortune is wrecked, faith, knowledge, and skill of hand" (*V*, 27).

Having made his point about real value, Barnes turns to the question of how commercial value is determined. This depends upon labor and upon the mutual experiences of workers, sellers, and buyers; each man's labor, too, is rated in the marketplace by its comparison with other labor that produces, or could produce, commodities or life-gear. The value of labor has a further set of determinants in the action of the body and mind on the work and the reaction of the body or mind to the work. In painting or the grinding of cutlery, there is the action of the body and the mind on the work and the reaction of the body to lead and inhaled steel dust. The shepherd's body and mind provides the work in the tending of sheep, but he might find a reaction to the work, such as loneliness, trying to his mind. Work to which the conscience reacts, Barnes points out, such as that of keeping a "house of ill-fame, the buying and selling of stolen goods, the adulteration of food and drink, and businesses in which great gain may be made by lying, and the deceiving of unwary people" will bring a "pernicious reaction to the conscience, and so to the soul" (V, 34).

In his essay "Exchange, etc.," Barnes makes some interesting points. First of all, he demonstrates that it is necessary for one people to sell as much to another nation as they buy from them; otherwise, the first group ends up with what modern economists call a balance of payments deficit. This balance is important to the economic life of a country, he says, "but this seemingly harmless truth may have become, in our dealings with China, a great evil and a great sin, since the Chinese have, from their own lands and hands, most of the kinds of life-gear that we could sell them from England, and so we push upon them the sale of a poison—opium" (V, 35). In this chapter, the add-on costs of transportation, as well as of any other handling or processing costs, are shown to affect the value of a commodity.

The chapter called "Compound Labour" seeks to anticipate objections to his earlier assertion that labor is the measure of commercial value. It is clear that labor is rewarded unequally for the same quantity of work. A factoryhand, for example, is not paid the same for a week's labor as is a watchmaker or a physician. The disparity arises because of the difference between simple and compound labor. Simple labor is that which demands little else save physical action—picking fruit, for instance, or loading boxes into trucks. Compound labor, on the other hand, involves the physical action plus other "quantities of labour" such as the acquisition of tools by a craftsman and "hand-skill" and "mind-skill." The teamster must be compensated for his skill and the use of his horses and equipment, and the physician must be paid for his education and training.

But there are other factors that affect the commercial value of a commodity as well; these four factors are called transferences of rating. First, there is the transference of rating from the labor which may have brought a commodity to hand to that which would bring its equal to hand. An example of this is a situation in which a farmer is offered a new handle for his rake at the price of ten units of labor when he knows that he can make one himself for only six units. In the farmer's mind, the rake handle is rated not by the labor which produced it, but by the labor that could produce its equal. Second, there is the transference of rating from the labor that a commodity takes to bring it to hand, that is, the price, to the labor that it will eliminate. If a carpenter is offered a new saw which would cost the equivalent of a thousand units of labor, and he determines that the tool will save him two thousand units in his work, then it is worth it to him to give the thousand units for the saw. The third transference of rating is one which Barnes calls the labor for which circumstances call on the buyer without it. A welcome reaction, such as a thirsty man's to a cool drink of water, can lead a person to place a higher value on a commodity or service than he otherwise might. A farmer without any seed at planting time will pay dearly to procure what he needs. Another form of this is the reaction to the rare, in which a person might put a very high value on the acquisition of the only known copy of a book or a particularly unusual gem. The fourth transference of rating is from the labor that produced a commodity to that which would bring another somewhat similar to the first. If a certain painting has a value of ten thousand units of labor and a second, which I like nearly as well cost only five thousand, I might choose the lesser of the two because the difference in price is much larger than the difference between my reaction to each.

Barnes's discussion of supply and demand is also based upon his conception of labor: "The supply of a commodity is the measure of the labour by which commodities are brought to hand; and demand for a commodity is the measure of the labour for which circumstances call on the buyer without it" (V, 48). If the wheat harvest is scant, for instance, the farmer still labors just as hard to produce it as he does in a year with a bumper crop; yet the fruits of his labor are less. Thus we can see that labor is the basis for supply. Similarly, demand for commodities is the labor which men are willing to give to procure such things; people will give more of their labor or the fruits of their labor for fuel during a cold winter than they might otherwise, for example.

True wealth is defined as "the happy use of a fulness of happily won or received life-gear" (V, 50). It is not money as such. Barnes cites the gold camps of Australia as a case in point. There, the stories go, men gave huge sums of gold for ordinary foodstuffs and articles of clothing, so an amount which might constitute wealth in England would be a much more modest sum in the gold fields. Here again, labor is the determinant: since a large segment of the work force spends its time looking for gold rather than producing clothing and foodstuffs, the value of the latter rises and that of the former falls. In a parenthetical discussion here, Barnes states his disapproval of the way in which English newspapers advertised for Australian emigrants. The wages for various occupations were given in terms of gold and not of the commercial value of the labor itself. Many people were thus misled and traveled to Australia with false hopes.

It is difficult for even the most disciplined person, let alone a clergyman, to discuss money and wealth without philosophizing, and Barnes is no exception. He warns against the evil uses of wealth, against the pursuit of wealth for its own sake, and against greed and miserliness. As an example of a people who eschewed the evils of wealth, Barnes gives his rendition of the history of Sparta. In an attempt to make his people hardy, toilsome, free, and brave, King Lycurgus gave the Spartans laws against luxury, idleness, the love of money, and fear of death. The people flourished under these rules until a law was passed which allowed men to hold monopolies of land and to hire others to work it. This led to the downfall of Sparta.

Monopolies and the tyrannies of capital Barnes sees as threats to the freedom of nineteenth-century English society. Freedom is of three forms: lawless, lawful, and circumstantial. Lawless freedom, or license, is freedom to do whatever a person wants to do. Here, there is too much freedom, even for a Nero or a Caligula, when he lives with other people. Lawful freedom is that which allows a person to do as he or she will within the constraints of the law. Circumstantial freedom is that under which a person may freely act without being limited by circumstances. For instance, the law may give everyone the right to vote for a representative in a governing body. However, if circumstances are such that a worker, should he or she decide to vote, will most certainly bring down the wrath of the employer, then the worker's freedom is limited by circumstance.

This circumstantial freedom is threatened by the centering of capital in a few hands, that is, in monopolies, especially when it leads to the use of the factory system. The hired factory hand gives up many potential choices when he takes a job; even his time is not his own since his movements are regulated by the factory whistle. Other choices have been removed, too. As long as one stays on at the factory, his choice of occupation is eliminated or at best severely restricted; the workman must attend to the task given to him or her by the person in charge. There is a lack of inducement for advancing one's station, too, under such a system. Barnes sees the independent tradesman or craftsman as being far better off in terms of circumstantial freedom, if not in every way, than his hired counterpart.

The factory system, in addition to limiting circumstantial freedom, contributes to the rise of crime in two important ways: first, the system by its very nature is dependent on a large work force that is concentrated near the plant site. This concentration leads to crowded living conditions, loss of privacy, and an atmosphere generally conducive to crime. Furthermore, most of the workers who have been forced into the system have had to leave the land, giving up their property. Statistics from the population figures of 1831 show that the prevalence of crime varies inversely with the average size of farms in the locality; areas with large farms—and fewer land owners—had more crime than areas with many small farms owned by more people. Barnes concludes from this that "the result is that the possession of property, whether to a large or small amount, retains a man from breaking the laws of his country" (V, 72). Too, the crime rates are shown to be higher in manufacturing areas than in agricultural ones; the rate goes even higher as the population of the factory towns increase.

While labor is seen to be at the basis for commercial value, it is difficult to arrive at a handy measure of labor. One way to measure labor is to look at its effect, the work produced. Yet this can be a false indicator because labor is both action and reaction and the work produced is the effect of only the action. For instance, it is one thing to shovel coal in the fresh air and sunshine but quite another to shovel it into a flaming furnace door in a hot, smoky basement. Again, drilling through ten feet of chalk is much easier than drilling through ten feet of granite. Time has been taken as a measure of labor instead of the work produced, but this, too, can be inaccurate. The intensity of labor in a given time may vary for any of a great number of reasons, the skill of the worker being only one. While Barnes recognizes that an equitable system of measuring work needs to be established, he does not suggest a specific one; he confines himself to writing about the more general aspects of the problem.

In many ways, Barnes is ahead of his time when he recognizes as a harmful working condition the state he calls the reaction of inaction on the mind and the body. He sees that certain workers—clerks and secretaries, for example—have little opportunity to engage in physical activities; this breeds weakness, irritability, and bad health in general. More important, he sees the danger of inaction of the mind, the familiar assembly-line syndrome of the twentieth century. A job which requires little thought and consists of repeating a series of simply physical tasks Barnes sees as leading to silliness, moodiness, and even madness. This effect of the division of labor in the factory system is a real evil, as modern industrial psychologists will attest. The elimination of tedium and the promotion of job satisfaction, Barnes knew, are important no less to the work as to the worker; to improve the lot of the worker is to improve the quality of the work.

The dignity of simple labor is a quality which was being lost in the often materialistic nineteenth-century English society. Occupations such as that of carpentry or farming were shunned as too difficult. Barnes describes the situation in the following terms:

> An intelligible rule for the esteem of callings would be that labour, which works most for the welfare of man, should be the most highly esteemed, and that those which only win wealth to the labourer without yielding a corresponding good to those from which the wealth is drawn, should be less esteemed; but there is no such rule, for a cunning and successful trader in the shares of swindling companies may be as much esteemed as a farmer, or builder, or weaver, or tanner. (V, 101)

To nineteenth-century English minds, at least, the respectability of a craft or profession was related directly to the amount of wealth which went along with it. If "Willie brew'd a peck o' ma't," it is less respected than the activities of the owner of a large brewery. Similarly, spinning flax on a cottage wheel is disreputable when compared with the running of a textile mill employing women and children for long hours under frightful conditions.

In his discussion of machinery, Barnes questions some of the assumptions underlying the factory system and the industrial revolution itself. While his subject is topical, many of his assertions sound very modern indeed. He states that the opinion that machines lessen labor and make it possible to produce for less labor or money than otherwise is not necessarily true. Machinery transfers rather than lessens labor. A machine is to labor what a battery is to electricity, that is, a means of storing and accumulating labor. The labor which went into making the machine, even the mining and smelting of ore for its metal parts and the cutting and sawing of trees for its wood, must be counted in its cost. This labor can be said to be "stored" in the machine for later use. Then it may be directed at a quantity of work at will, and the machinery will carry out its tasks in a shorter time than it would take to do the same work by hand; in this is its advantage. If the total amount of work produced by the machine is larger than the amount "stored"—the machine's true cost—then it is advantageous to build and to use it, it would seem. But, of course, there are other factors, such as the quality of a machine-made product versus that of an object made by hand. Moreover, there is the effect of the machine on the health of the workman's mind or body. If a skilled craftsman is replaced by a machine he must tend by turning a crank every thirty seconds, the effect on his mind is likely to be harmful. Some machinery, especially that of the nineteenth century with its lack of industrial health and safety regulations, could be physically dangerous as well, causing broken bones, loss of limbs, and even death. All these factors, Barnes says, must be taken into consideration before a determination of the value of machinery can be made. We should not blindly invoke the name of progress and the public good when a manufacturer proposes to build a "fifty-windowed" factory which would put skilled craftsmen out of business. It seems that every factory owner is working for the public when he wants an accommodation from the working class, but he is a private citizen with a right to manage his business as he sees fit when an accommodation is asked of him (*V,* 108).

The factory system relies on labor congregated in large groups which Barnes sees as an evil. In addition to the points discussed earlier on the subject, poor conditions, lack of privacy, and the rise of crime rates, he demonstrates that crowded factories lead to "clock-thralldom" or the pressure to work constantly all day without breaks or slowdowns. The larger the factory, the greater the pressure, since fifteen minutes respite given to ten workers is not nearly as expensive as a five-minute break given to thousands. Mob action is another danger—two thousand workers rising up against authority is a greater threat than the isolated group of ten or twenty. Finally, the fast growing populations of the cities act as a weapon against religion. The close-knit parishes of the countryside do not exist in the teeming tenement districts of the industrial cities.

The treatment of the poor was a problem, too, in the rapidly changing society of the nineteenth century. Barnes condemns the system then in use of paying or caring for the unemployed, saying that it is an evil to the community and to the poor man himself for him to receive money through the poor laws for nothing other than the fact that he needs it. A laborer should receive payment for what he has done, Barnes asserts, and not for what circumstances he is in. The poor laws were predicated on two ideas. First, that it will aid those who are productive if competition for their labor is removed, and second, that it is necessary to pay the idle poor since there is no work by which they can earn their livings. He objects to both of these. To the first, he says that in this system the necessities of life consumed by the idle are produced by the productive, so that both groups exist upon the labor of one. This does not seem advantageous. To the second idea, Barnes says that it is always better for both the taxed citizenry and the paupers if the poor do something rather than nothing for the money they receive.

Did the poor receivers of the four millions of pounds of poor's rate in the year 1848 do every conceivable bit of work by which their hands could have contributed aught to the welfare of their neighbors? Is the last church path in the kingdom gravelled and thoroughly clean? Is the last stile freed of muddiness? Is the last yard of parish road mended and drained? Is the last brook cleared of the last obstacle which drove its gritty waters needlessly over the wide fields? (V, 176)

And the work produced would be not more valuable than the reaction of the worker to the labor. Each could receive his pay with dignity, knowing that he had toiled well and had been productive.

Barnes's concern in the poor laws is a topical one. The Poor Law Amendment Act of 1834 which revised the treatment of the poor, was based on a commission report's specific recommendations. The

recommendations—although they took years to put into effect—
included an overhaul of the workhouses and the abolition of the
Speenhamland system, whereby poor relief was used to supplement
wages. The amount of relief was based on need although in no case
was the aid exorbitant.

Historical Interests

If Barnes's approach to contemporary social and economic problems seems broad, it is probably because of the perspective his
lifelong study of history provided him. Besides his well-known
interests in linguistic and literary history, he also examined many
other facets of the past; his aim was a broad understanding of the
history of human culture. This goal led him to the study of architecture, archeology, and paleontology. Some of his early contributions to the *Gentleman's Magazine* were on these subjects, several
being illustrated with his own woodcuts.[2] He wrote histories and
descriptions of standing churches in the area, but also described
various ruins and fallen structures in his publications. Recent history, too, did not escape his attention; 1832 saw the publication
in Hone's yearbook of Barnes's comments on regional customs, some
of which were doubtlessly passing away.[3] He published, too, his
opinions of the Kimmeridge coal money.[4] A number of ring-shaped
stones were found at some prehistoric mining sites; these obviously
hand-hewn specimens were taken by some to be forms of coins used
by the native tribes in the time before the Roman occupation. Barnes
was of the opinion that the shards were not money at all but rather
turnings from a crude lathe. These publications were based on his
interest in regional history, especially in those aspects which concerned the preservation of artifacts from preindustrial life. These
could help modern society to see what the past had been like;
perhaps, he thought, the best of what had been abandoned might
be restored once it was known. In this way, the past might help
to build a better future. While this primitivism is based largely on
a myth of a glorious past, it was nonetheless in line with the
backward looks men like Ruskin, Pater, and Arnold were taking.

Barnes's retained an interest in antiquarianism throughout his
life. He helped found the Dorset County Museum, an institution
dedicated to the preservation of historical artifacts from the region.
Impetus for the formation of the museum was provided by an un-

likely source—the London to Dorchester railway. In 1845, an announcement by the South Western Railway that it would lay track through to Dorchester prompted citizens to voice concern over the effects of the construction. While geologists were excited about the prospect of uncovering many fossils, others, including Barnes, were afraid that the track-laying would destroy heretofore undiscovered historical treasures. The result was a compromise culminating in the cooperation of the railway in the preservation of historical sites and the founding of the Dorset County Museum. Barnes was elected secretary of the organization and remained in this capacity for many years.

The Dorset Natural History and Archeological Field Club was founded in 1871 after some urging by Barnes. This group toured the countryside, examining spots of historical and geological interest. Artifacts collected on their trips were often placed in the museum as well as drawings and photographs—or sun-prints as Barnes called them—of interesting structures. The club also held meetings at which papers were read by members and others. Several papers on historical topics were given by Barnes to this group and others, including the British Archeological Association.

Barnes's approach to history is as broad and as catholic as his approaches to other disciplines. The methodology is based on an examination of four kinds of evidence: first, the physical evidence, his own observations of ruins, barrows, roads, and so on; second, the linguistic evidence, the etymologies of place names, for example; third, the historical documents, the comments of the ancient historians, legal documents and records; fourth, the literary evidence, the poetry, songs and sagas of the people involved.

His first book-length historical study came out in 1858 and is a good example of how Barnes uses the available evidence to prove a base for his assertions. *Notes on Ancient Britain and the Britons* is a look at the principal group inhabiting Britain during the early Middle Ages: the Celts—or Britons, to use Barnes's term. The Saxons, as the Britons' foes and eventual usurpers, and the modern-day Welsh, as descendents of the Britons, are discussed as well. A glance at the table of contents gives the impression that the author is using a shotgun approach, peppering his audience with pellets of information; a chapter on food is followed by a chapter on exercise and by one entitled "What was the Cardinal or head Sky-point with the Britons? the East?" The history seems to lack organization. But close examination shows that Barnes is presenting the Britons through the triad, a traditional Celtic rhetorical form: first, he looks at their physical state and describes food, shelter, clothing, and activity; then he examines their organizational state and discusses their laws and customs; third, he studies their spiritual and philosophic state, and comments on their religion, their language, and their literature.

Early in the first section of the physical state of the Britons, Barnes discusses food. He uses an old Welsh proverb as evidence for the use of acorns as food by the Celts and then goes on to provide a discussion of their possible use of various nuts and berries. At one point, he recounts how a local dentist who wished to find out about tooth decay among the Britons opened one of the barrows in the hills surrounding Dorchester. There he found a skeleton and "a quantity of hard brittle stuff, which was of a hue not unlike that of peat, and which he deemed to be the contents of the colon."[5] The dentist pounded some of the material and found that it contained seeds which the dentist, being of a scientific bent, planted. After a few weeks the seed yielded plants which proved to be raspberries. From this first hand evidence, Barnes was able to conclude that the Celts in Britain ate wild raspberries. He also consults historical documents in this section, quoting Caesar's descriptions of British housing and boatmaking. He agrees with Herodian's theory of the reasons why the early Briton tattooed his body—it was for decoration and not, as Caesar had surmised, for scaring his enemies. Linguistic evidence is used throughout the first section, as well as literary remains. In the chapter on burial, for example, he cites an ancient Welsh saying to prove that burial in barrows was disapproved of after the coming of Christianity.

Barnes also deals with the laws, customs, and social organization of the Britons. He uses linguistic evidence as well as his own observations to show that some of the ancient roads which were thought to be built by the Romans were actually built by the Britons. A discussion of surviving place names leads him to the assertion that there was much more water in the form of lakes, ponds, and marshes in England in those times than there is now. Historical authorities are used here, too. The Welsh Triads are used to document what he says about British law, and the Venerable Bede is invoked in his discussion of Saxon law.

At the end of the second section, Barnes includes an interesting chapter entitled "British Treatment of Crime" which deals less with the historical aspects of this subject—he has covered this in other places—than with contemporary questions regarding it. In this essay, he makes a plea for abolishing the present system of punishment and advocates replacing it with the British-Saxon method. This method involves a trial to determine guilt much as the modern system, but once guilt is established, the old way demands that the prisoner make full restitution, or in Barnes's words, right the wrong. This restitution could take many forms, but it would always fit the crime. Barnes was evidently so taken by the idea when he was writing about it that he felt an uncontrollable urge to proselytize immediately.

The last section of the history deals with the religion, the language, and the literature of the early Britons. The Celts honored the arts and learning to the extent that they established a national school of poetry and music.[6] Again, Barnes uses various kinds of evidence in making his arguments, but his main source here is the literary documents themselves, especially the Welsh Triads. While many phenomena in the spiritual and physical worlds are naturally grouped in threes—the present, the past, the future; the three primary colors; the Christian Trinity; earth, heaven, hell—the Celtic mind seems more attracted to "the threeness of things," Barnes says, than are other minds. Thus it was natural for the Druids and teachers of the Britons to deliver their messages in divinity, law, and art in clusters of three called *trioedd,* or "threenesses." This format was a great aid to memory, as well. The Triads served as the Briton's history, their law, and their repository of customs. Barnes sees the composition of this collection of wisdom as taking place over the centuries, "as there was a call for them in the gathering of new facts or the teaching of new doctrines."[7] The Triads were a reflection of the race and Barnes uses them to support generalities he makes about the early British people.

The religion of the Britons Barnes extrapolates from the Triads. The Celts believed in the transmigration of souls from one state or circle of being to another. The three states of being for man are "earthlife," *abred,* and *gwynved; abred* is the circle of evil, *gwynved* that of happiness. It is man's lot to live on earth, to fall to a state of *abred,* and then to transmigrate back to earthlife. As the process goes on, man learns what he must do to avoid the three things which cause him to enter *abred:* a disregard of knowledge, a slighting of the good, and a love of evil. Then he is ready to earn *gwynved,* or happiness.

Barnes cites the classical historians here, too, such as Caesar and Tertullian. He also uses personal observations, as when he describes Stonehenge and other "Druid circles" in Dorset and neighboring counties. He shows a remarkable firsthand knowledge of his subject in his discussion of barrows, or tumuli. These he divides into two types, *carneddau* or burial mounds and *crugau* or session mounds, and is able to distinguish between the two by their structures. Extensive linguistic evidence is used in a section on place names in which Barnes attempts to deduce the identities of the original inhabitants or settlers of various districts by an analysis of the surviving name.

Another attempt at early English historiography is *Early England and the Saxon-English,* published in 1869. Barnes relies heavily on historical documents for his recounting of the wars between the Saxon invaders and the Britons, but he is careful to consult the histories of both sides. For example, he might give the *Anglo-Saxon Chronicle* version of a battle or event and then turn to Aneurin or Taliesin or another Welsh bard for his account. This is necessary for an accurate report, Barnes believed:

> For the history of the struggles of the Saxon-English with the Britons, we have been wont to take only the Saxon-English without the Welsh writings; but, as we know that, in later wars, the men of each side make the best of their own deeds, and the truth stands partly with both sides rather than wholly with either of them, so it is likely that the truth of the Saxon-English settlements may be shown more clearly through the blended Welsh and English writings than by the words of only either the Saxon or Briton.[8]

Once he has recounted the history of the Saxon-British wars, Barnes goes on to describe Saxon society in the various English settlements. In the section "Saxon-English Laws," he discusses the political organization of the settlers, the basis of which was the *Burh,* or borough. The borough consisted of a group of ten men tied together under the law. These ten men were responsible for one another and for each others' families even in the event of crime. If one man broke the law and fled, the nine were to bring him in within a month to answer for his crime or else to answer for it themselves. These boroughs, or tithings, were themselves bound together in groups of ten called hundreds, which have survived in one form or another until the present. Various Anglo-Saxon laws are recounted in this section not only, it seems, for the sake of the historical record, but also as a comparison with contemporary jurisprudence.

The social organization of the Saxons is recounted in a section entitled "Landholding and Ranks of Men." Trade, the food of the Saxons, their clothing, and amusements are treated as well. Two chapters, "Heathenhood" and "Christianity," trace the history of Saxon religion. Barnes likens the pagan religion of the Teutonic Saxons to that of other pantheistic creeds like the Roman. The history of Christianity in non-Celtic Britain is traced from the landing of Augustine until well into the Middle Ages.

"The English Language" is a history of the language for the nonlinguist. Barnes gives an example of Old English, which he calls Saxon-English, from the Bible; an example of Middle English, which he calls Old English, from Chaucer; and examples of evolving modern English from Wycliffe and Tyndale in an attempt to show that "The English has come on to us, changing by slow wear, or wilful word-changings, to the form in which we now speak it."[9] The familiar plea for the purgation of words of Latinate derivation is given as well as the list of words with their preferred Saxon counterparts—"anticipate," *forween;* "decimate," *offtithen;* "eclipse," *swarthen,* and so on.

The Frisians or the "fatherstock" of the Saxons, are treated in a separate section; their history is recounted by tracing them to tribes mentioned by Tacitus and Caesar. Barnes looks to the *Anglo-Saxon Chronicle* and to Geoffrey of Monmouth for evidence linking the Frisians with the Saxon settlers of England. Using his own knowledge of Old English and several linguistic documents of the Frisian language, he is able to establish an apparent direct relationship. Putting the historical and linguistic evidence together, Barnes concludes that the Frisians, the Angles, and the Saxons are all one.

In *Notes on Ancient Britain and the Britons* and *Early England and the Saxon English,* Barnes offers histories of the two groups inhabiting England during the early Middle Ages. These histories are not the specialized ones of the linguist, say, or of the political scientist, but rather resemble the work of the cultural historian in that their scope is broad. Barnes tries to examine his subject from as many points of view as possible; by studying each of the parts he seeks to discover the whole. His methodology follows this broad approach as well, bringing to bear as many kinds of evidence as he can instead of relying on a single type. Again and again he cites his personal observation of ancient structures and artifacts, the accounts of earlier historians, surviving records and documents, linguistic evidence, and the accounts of early literature.

There is a didactic side to Barnes's history—not surprising, perhaps, in a nineteenth-century schoolmaster and preacher—but it is much more evident in his shorter work in periodicals than in the book-length histories. In an article in *Macmillan's* entitled "The Rise and Progress of Trial by Jury in Britain,"[10] fully half of the text is devoted to legal reform in the contemporary world. British foreign policy comes under the gun often in the guise of an example in an argument that has nothing to do with current events or foreign affairs. The expansionist policy in India heads the list in this category, followed closely by the opium trade with China. Pet causes like spelling reform and English purism, too, are often introduced into discussions of other subjects.

The historical works stand up surprisingly well in the light of modern scholarship. Here and there the author makes a wrong turn because he misreads a signpost, but most often he is on the right track. His success is due to a painstaking attention to detail as well as to an unwillingness to disregard any information no matter how difficult it is to acquire. Admittedly an amateur, Barnes nonetheless completed his tasks with scholarly thoroughness.

Chapter Five

Aesthetics and Education

Barnes's Aesthetics

Any artist worthy of the name develops—however loosely—an aesthetic theory, a sense of what art is, what it does, and what the role of the artist is in its creation. Barnes's aesthetic theory is an amalgamation of several points of view; his varied interests and occupations make this almost unavoidable. His great love, of course, was poetry and the study of literature, but other avocations color his thinking on this subject as well. As a graphic artist—he produced many woodcuts and watercolors—he knew the importance of color, design, and perspective. His accomplishments as an amateur musician led to the formulation of his beliefs on harmonic proportions, and these ideas were bolstered by his study of physics. Finally, Barnes was a teacher and a clergyman, these vocations doubtlessly having a profound influence on his thoughts on art.

The aim of art is the pursuit and interpretation of the beautiful, according to the Dorset poet.[1] The beautiful is defined in two ways: first, the beautiful in nature is the unmarred result of God's first creative or forming will; the beautiful in art, on the other hand, is the result of man working in accordance with the beautiful in nature.

God's forming will results in two types of phenomena which may be called work and after-work. Work is the direct result of His creative will; after-work comes when a prior work in His forming will has begun to be marred, or altered. For example, when a pea is planted, the root sprouts, and soon a plant grows out of the ground. This is the result of God's creative will, this is "work." If after a few days, however, a gardener comes along and cuts off the young plant, he is altering or marring God's work. If in a week or so two plants grow back where there was only one before, this is called "after-work." The after-work would not have appeared had the work not been altered in the first place. God's first formative or creative will causes, then, the full flowering of goodness; after-work, itself also a product of God's will, fills in the losses of goodness which may occur.

We do not find most of God's works in the full beauty of His first forming will. Man may be marred by his vices or evil deeds, by overwork, by unfavorable living conditions, or other factors detrimental to his physical, mental, or moral health. Similarly, a plant or animal might be uncared for or mistreated, thus causing it to grow stunted or to become diseased. "Still," Barnes says, "in plants, animals, and man, and in the world, there is yet so much of the beauty of God's primary work, that our minds can well rise from their marred shapes to the higher ones, or the beau ideal, of which they may be spoilt forms, and that beau ideal is, in our opinion, one of the true objects of art."[2]

We are able to gather from an observation of choice forms enough of beauty to project the ideal, or at least to conceive it. The artist, the Raphael or Michelangelo, is able to imagine what the ideal looks like and then to portray it in the sculpture or on the canvas. The true artist trains himself to recognize beauty wherever it is, even in the meanest, most mundane surroundings. The artistic person looks for, among other things, beauty of form and proportion.

Fitness or harmony produces beauty of form and proportion. This fitness, according to Barnes, and strength are determinants of quantity. In addition, we recognize fitnesses or harmonies of number and of curves.

Quantity refers to the proportion of the size of one thing to another. For instance, a man with legs twice as long as he needs would be adjudged ungainly; on the other hand, a woman with arms too short to carry out simple tasks would be looked upon as being unfit. God's rule of work, according to Barnes, is "none to leave, and none to lack." In other words, God's first formative will dictates that proportions will be just right, not too much as to cause a waste, and not too little as to cause a want.

This rule of no waste no want should be a pattern for us whenever we are producing something, be it a picture, a building, or a haircut. A heavy roof supported by slender pillars would not be handsome in that the effect of the impression given is one of unsteadiness. On the other side, a thick marble base on a coatrack would be ridiculous because of its obvious waste of strength and material.

Another fitness of things is that of number. The number two is important to life-forms, Barnes says, because we can easily see that we should have two arms and two legs and that birds and insects need two wings. The need for two ears, too, is obvious, and the stereoscope and other optical devices prove the need for two eyes. Another part of the fitness of number is a theory Barnes calls "Harmonic Proportion," or the harmonic triad. He explains the idea in the following:

As to Harmonic Proportion, three quantities are in Harmonic Proportion when the first bears the same proportion to the third as the difference between the first and the second bears to the difference between the second and third. 6, 3, 2, are a harmonic threeness, for the first, 6, is three times 2 (the third) and the difference between 6 and 3 is 3 which is three times the difference between 3 and 2 which is thus, $6:2 ::(6 - 3):(3 - 2)$.

To find the harmonic third to two given numbers, multiply the first by the second, and divide the product by twice the first minus the second. To find the harmonic third to 6 and 3 as foregiven, $6 \times 3 = 18$. $2 \times 6 = 12 - 3 = 9$. Divide 18 by $9 = 2$. If you have any two of the three you may find the other by other formulae. Of course, the harmonic third is often fractional.[3]

Barnes found harmonic proportion useful in a number of ways, in architecture and interior design, for instance, as well as in such mundane areas as bookbinding and picture framing.

Curves, symbols of motion, Barnes finds as another fitness. The curve occurs naturally, and therein lies its beauty. The very sky is curved as are the sun and the moon, the rainbow, leaves and flowers, and the flight-paths of birds. The act of throwing a stone or hitting a ball produces a curve of the truest form; in Newton's time, when scientists used his new calculus to try to find the curve of least resistance, they found that it already existed in nature as the head of a fish. The curve imparts a natural beauty, Barnes believed, possibly because it is a manifestation of the creative will of God.

Nature, Barnes says, is the best school of art, and the best art students are those who are nature's best interpreters. To learn about color, then, and which colors blend harmoniously, one must look to nature. Looking at nature, he concludes that nature rarely contrasts warm and cold colors. He comments, too, on the fact that strong colors which are juxtaposed in nature often are shaded with tints of one another, are reconciled by a common touch of black, or are each lightened with a touch of white.

The beauty of landscape arises from its natural harmony; the greens of the earth and the blue of the sky, for instance, are more soothing to the eye than a blinding world of red and white. The forms, too, of hills, trees, and rivers blend in the natural landscape to create a sense of beauty. But the aesthetic response to landscape is not limited to the visual stimulus; Barnes says,

> In all these beautiful things there is fitness—fitness of water to irrigate growth, and to run for all lips to the sea; fitness of land to take and send onward the stream; fitness of strength to weight, and of the stem to the head of a tree; fitness of elasticity to force, as that of the poplar, and the bough whose very name is bending, and bulrush and the grass to the wind; fitness of protection to life, as in the armed holly and thorn, and the bush, or ditch-guarded epilbium; and a harmony of the whole with the good of man.[4]

Barnes appreciates the beauty of physical forces acting and responding in accordance with the laws of nature, as well as the attractiveness of the idea that everything in nature exists for a purpose.

Moral beauty can be recognized also. God's primary will yields only good work, as we have seen, and yet this work is capable of being corrupted by evil or vice. Any attempt by man to restore God's original intention, any attempt to right a wrong even in the face of overwhelming odds and certain failure, Barnes sees as beautiful. Art, since its aim is the pursuit and interpretation of the beautiful in God's world, can make much use of this moral beauty.

Barnes comments on the rise of art among the people of the cities, referring to new styles of art and architecture being patronized at the time by the newly wealthy middle class. He sees art—especially public art such as decorative friezes on buildings and statues in parks—as being restorative to the overworked laboring classes. While this bit of naiveté indicates an isolation from the often desperate plight of the urban poor, his remarks on taste and the lack of it are much in line with those of writers like Matthew Arnold and John Ruskin:

> The old workmen were faithful and wrought to God, or art or conscience, rather than to Pluto. They finished their work fore and aft, not more for the outside crown than for the eyes and soul of the worshipper. Their stone was stone; their oak was oak; their iron metal. But our age is one of falsehood and sham; we have deal painted and veneered into an imitation

of more costly wood; brick under white plaster, feigning stone; a worse metal washed with a film of a better one; cloth shown to neighbours for leather; paste for gems; imitations instead of nature's truth.[5]

There will be no high art when the workman or artist panders to low taste or deceives his fellows. The study of art should give the mind a keener insight into the beauties of nature; it teaches us to see. And the artist has an obligation to pass on this skill of perception, to lend his mind in its perception of beauty to another, as Robert Browning points out in "Fra Lippo Lippi." The object of art, Barnes says, is the doing of good to men's minds, not the acquisition of money; the high aim of the artist should be the winning of excellence, the spring from which all true rewards flow.

In many ways, Barnes's aesthetic ideas are typical of Victorian England; follow nature, he exhorts the artist, for nature is the manifestation of the primary creative force. The artist is seen as the interpreter of beauty, the one who passes on his or her insights to the less inspired. Art is in danger of being corrupted and even destroyed by those who would exploit it for money, the sham artist, the mass producers, the inferior craftsmen. Finally, he asks those engaged in art not to forget the high aim of their profession, the pursuit and interpretation of the beautiful in God's works.

The Scientific Works

When he discusses the beauty of nature, as we have seen, Barnes is concerned with something more than just sensory beauty; his observation of nature elicits in him an essentially aesthetic response to what he calls harmony. This quality can be characterized as an obedience to the laws of nature. When the wind blows at a certain velocity, the oak responds in one way, the poplar in another; tall grass waves in one predictable pattern, and the sea in another. Even the uninspired, dirty, and noisy railroad train, when it demonstrates harmonious obedience to the laws of physics, is beautiful. "A train was going off in a curve, and its form slowly lessening, while its angular speed was increasing by the bend in the curve, till at last, by another turn, it shrank slowly to a speck, without any seeming speed, when a lady alongside exclaimed, 'How beautiful is motion!' "[6]

Barnes's attraction to science began early, not surprisingly, when he was a school teacher. While living at Chantry House when he was master of the school at Mere, he even put his scientific knowledge to practical use through inventions he fabricated himself. He made a quadrant of his own design as well as an instrument to describe ellipses.

As a schoolmaster, Barnes was dissatisfied with many of the textbooks available at the time, so accordingly, he set out to write many of his own. His dissatisfaction stemmed from the fact that he believed that minds should be trained and not merely crammed with facts, that the school curriculum should contain the germs of all the knowledge an educated person would need to live a happy and productive life. As a part of this thinking, his ideas on science were prominent: he believed that an understanding of science was important to other branches of learning as well as valuable in developing the powers of reason and observation. His object was to make the study of science not only understandable but interesting, so that his students' acquaintanceship with science would not end when they left the classroom.

His daily teaching routine was an attempt to integrate several subject areas while holding the attention of students from various educational levels. He usually gave a lecture on science during the first hour, varying the subject from day to day; one lecture might be spent on botany, another on geology, physics, electricity, chemistry, natural history, or zoology. This lecture, which usually began with a demonstration of principles or specimens, was given by the teacher. Following this, the students were required to write a composition from their notes, taking care to observe the rules of organization, grammar, and spelling. In the afternoon, the lesson was usually continued with a field trip. The students might follow a lecture on botany with a walk in the country where they collected specimens of various plants; if the subject was natural history or geology, they would arm themselves with hammers and collection bags and comb the rock outcroppings of the nearby hills for fossils or minerals.[7]

In an attempt to make available materials which were compatible with his teaching theories and methods, Barnes published a series of books on various subjects which were used as texts by his students. The books had other readers, of course, but one of the major aims of his publishing efforts was pedagogical; his knowledge was only valuable if it could be disseminated.

Most of his scientific work was published between 1834 and 1847, the year of his ordination, beginning with *A Few Words on the*

Advantages of a More Common Adoption of the Mathematics as a Branch of Education, published by Whittaker and Company at London. It must be noted that Barnes's interest in scientific education came very early in comparison with other educators. One of his students, J. B. Lock, went on to become senior fellow, assistant tutor, and lecturer in mathematics and physics at Cambridge. Lock, commenting on Barnes's science lectures, says, "It seems worth recalling that such lectures are now given in most of the great public schools, in which such subjects were still untaught much less than thirty years ago."[8] Until the middle of the century, very little science was taught in the schools or universities. In fact, it was only in the last decades of the nineteenth century that British schools reached the level of continental schools in scientific and technical education, and this was achieved over the vehement objections of some of the most prominent humanists of the time. It is ironic, then, that some thirty to forty years before it was common to think so, a country poet was pressing for the adoption of mathematical and scientific education in the nation's schools.

Barnes followed his plea with *A Mathematical Investigation of the Principle of Hanging Doors, Gates, Swing Bridges, and Other Heavy Bodies,* published in 1835 by Simmonds and Sydenham in Dorchester. In 1841 Whittaker brought out *An Arithmetical and Commercial Dictionary,* a practical guide for students. Another science textbook was published in 1844, called *Exercises in Practical Science, Containing the Main Principles of Dynamics, Statics, Hydrostatics, and Hydrodynamics.* His *Outlines of Geography and Ethnography for Youth,* published in Dorchester in 1847, is a typical example of his textbook style. This book contains not only maps and names of places but attempts to combine the elements of physical and descriptive geography with studies of various human cultures. Here, as in his lectures at school, he blends dry facts with more interesting material to make the facts palatable to young intellectual appetites.

Rede-Craft, or Logic

Late in his life, Barnes brought out a work which combined two aims which were important to him: the instruction of the unschooled, and the promotion of his Saxon or Teutonic English. The subject was logic and it was Barnes's intention to teach it to "some homely men who may not have taken up logic at the University, nor have been led through Euclid's *Elements* at school, and may not have to wrangle Latin, with three opponents, on a thesis, in the schools."[9] These people, though uneducated, needed logic because there was so much unsound reasoning being foisted off on the English public, according to the author: "There is much of thinking among us and given forth in print such, that, if the writers of it had kept more closely to the calls of good logic, it might have taken a sounder shape, and there is much unsound reasoning of persuasion by which readers, who could try it by the light of sound redeship, would not be so easily misled" (*RC,* v). The public, even the uneducated, should be given the means to analyze and assess the information, arguments, and statistics being given to them; this is imperative for a free society and for the self-interest of the laboring classes. Of course, this thinking is right in line with Barnes's social theory.

He knew, too, that the presentation of the material in his logic primer must be appropriate for his audience. This is why, he says, he writes his book in Teutonic English, so that those who "seek an insight into rede-craft" will have it "outshown in English with English lore-words (terms of science)" (*RC,* v). Those who were not trained in Latin and Greek, he reasoned, would have trouble understanding the terms used in standard philosophical logic. He sought to alleviate this problem by the use of words and phrases more readily understood by an unsophisticated audience.

Rede-craft he defines as logic, or the art of reasoning, and wrangling is a wrestling with the mind or with words, another word for disputation or argument. His teaching of the structure of logic and its operations is fairly standard, but it is his language which makes the book seem odd, at least at first. He does retain the standard terminology for reference as when he defines "Speech-matters":

Speech-matters (praedicabilia) are:

1. *Kind* (genus)
2. *Hue* (species)
3. *Odds* (differentia)
4. *Selflihood* (proprium)
5. *Haplihood* (accident) (*RC,* 1)

In spite of the oddity of language, he teaches the standard logical instruction. The following, the beginning of his comments on the syllogism, is a good example of the way in which Barnes changes the nomenclature of logic so that it conforms to his Saxon English; at the same time, he used intact the system of logic standard in his day.

> Wrangling is mostly done by syllogism, a three-stepped rede-ship of three thought-puttings.
>
>   1. The *head* or *first step* (major propositio)
>   2. The *under* or *middle step* (minor propositio), and
>   3. The *upshot* or *last step* (conclusio), as—
>
>   1. "All men are breathesome."
>   2. "John is a man,"
>   3. So, "John is breathesome."
>
> The first-two steps are called together *fore-puttings* or *fore-steps* (prae-missi), and are put as true, whether they are so or not, or else as fore-begged and yielded. (*RC,* 23–24)

The volume was not well received. Although it is a competent enough introduction to logic, the language was judged to be extreme and unnecessary. While it might be pointed out that the language Barnes is proposing to replace is scarcely less specialized or confusing than his Saxon English, nonetheless his experiment failed to win popularity. The professional logicians and philosophers would be expected to reject *Rede-Craft,* but there is no record, either, of a wave of support from the book's intended audience.

The Literary Scholar and Critic

By the 1860s, when Barnes was no longer a schoolmaster, a large part of his writing was still done in the instructive mode. We find him especially interested in the history and theory of literature, digging in the cairns and barrows of archaic writings and then reporting on his findings in articles for various magazines and journals. His audience had changed, but the methodology was the same as he had used as a teacher: he educated himself and then sought to pass on what he had learned.

His "Rariora of Old Poetry" is a good example of his informational pieces. Published in *Macmillan's* in 1863, the piece is a survey of poetry in the bardic tradition. In it he discusses some observed relationships between classical dramatic and odic poetry and the dances and songs of certain aboriginal tribes of his own time such as the Iroquois and Hurons, the Polynesian Tonhas, and the African Kafirs. From these similarities he concludes that people have an innate attraction for song, drama, and poetry. The bard, a position or occupation which developed from the need to preserve the tribal lore, became important; the person holding this position was elevated—many times even becoming a noble—in the ancient tribes. The change in status of the poet over the years was a natural process, by Barnes's account:

> The art was, like man himself, leaning to lower aims, *prona in deferius,* though wise men and bards themselves as the British bards by their canons of bardship—did their best to preserve it as an instrument or good; but the more it degenerated, the less honour had the bard even of high-aiming song. Thus, whereas, in the time of Hoel Dda, the social rank of the bard was near that of the King; now, when the muse has been so often pandered to the low tastes which she ought to have refined, the place of the poet is only where he can hold himself by his birth, his wealth, or his earnings.[10]

Barnes traces the development of poetry through the centuries from the primitive days, when dance, song, drama, and poetry were all one and inexorably linked to religion and nature, to medieval times after which the bardic tradition died out. His "rariora" is a true collection of literary rarities with each tidbit supplying a link in the chain of development. Examples are given of poetry written by Prosper of Aquitaine, Proba Falconia, Juvencus, and other early Christian poets. He treats Teutonic poetry, demonstrating the differences between its prosody and that of the classical tongues. His familiarity with this school he attributes to the study of such works as *Judith, Beowulf, Pier's Plowman,* and the *Canterbury Tales* as well as the writings of Caedmon, Cynewulf, and King Alfred. Celtic poetry is represented, too, with a description of its particular versification and examples from representative triplets and *englyns.*

The oral tradition as a transmitter of history is discussed in "On the Credibility of Old Song-History and Tradition."[11] While the old British bards recognized three kinds of memorials—tradition or tongue; song or verse; and writing—only the last survived as a recognized instrument of history. There is an inherent danger, Barnes warns, in this belief. He maintains that tradition and verse can be disproved. His logic is simple: "while the belief that a tongue-tale or song-history may be true, may lead to the discovery that it is, the belief that it is false may stop in the holding of the falsehood of it, even while it may be true; and thus unbelief may be of more harm to historic truth than may be a keen faith."[12]

The reason for modern distrust of the oral tradition is not because it has been proved unreliable, but rather that we no longer use it to record our own history. If we look to the early poems of the Greeks, to the verse of the Celtic or Teutonic people, or to the dance-songs of modern-day aboriginal peoples, we see that the main use of poetry is as an instrument of history, the means by which the gathered wisdom of people is handed down from generation to generation.

In keeping with this purpose, various linguistic devices were employed by the keepers of the tradition as memory locks or aids to insure the integrity of the information. Time measures, accent, time, breathsound (vowel) rhyme, clipping (consonant) rhyme, and word-matching are all poetic devices Barnes identifies as memory locks. Some of these devices can become quite intricate, like the Welsh *cynghanedd* or consonantal rhyme. An example is the line "Dinas fawr dan nos o fwg." In each of the halves of this line, *DiNaS Fawr* and *DaN noS Fwg*, the sounds of *D, N, S,* and *F* occur in order, thus locking in the verse. It would be difficult to err and change the words of the line without changing the *cynghanedd*.

Another memory aid is the Hebrew device of resumption in which every line is begun with the same sound, as in the Hebrew of Psalm 119. Here we find every verse of the first part beginning with *aleph;* each verse of the second begins with *beth;* each in their third with *gimel,* and so on through the alphabet. In some forms of Irish and Persian poetry, we can see that a convention calls for words of one syllable to be used in a certain position in a line, words of two syllables in another place, and so on. A variation of this is the setting of the same word or sets of words at a particular position in the poem. These devices and others helped to insure that the information transmitted by the tradition remained stable.

Most of the mnemonic aids coexisted, for a time at least, with written languages indicating that the oral tradition does not die out immediately when writing is introduced to a culture. Both the Celtic Britons and the Teutonic tribes had writing for hundreds of years before the memorized verses were written down. This leads Barnes to conclude that there was a great deal of trust given to the oral tradition by the people that it served. Another indication of confidence in the tradition is demonstrated by the Bible:

> The locks of Hebrew verse are that of clipping, rhyme, and the athnach or measure pause, and thought matching or parallelism; and the firmness of that form, and the trust that was worthily put in it, is shown by some of the historical songs of the Bible, and first by that very old piece of verse by Lamech in Gen. iv. 23 and 24. Where great events are to be recorded they were put under the locks of verse as in the song of Moses and the children of Israel, with Miriam and the woman, in Exodus xv.; the glorious piece of Hebrew poetry, the Song of Moses, Deut. xxxii.; David's lamentation over Saul and Jonathan, 2 Sam. i.; and the Song of Deborah and Barak, Judges v.[13]

Barnes would not, however, have us accept at face value everything which is handed down through oral tradition, but he insists that it be taken seriously as a bona fide instrument of history. It is illogical, he says, to accept one people's account of a war because it is written down and at the same time reject the history given by the other side because it is transmitted through memory and the voice. The real history can probably be constructed by the comparison of the two along with the collation of other information such as the accounts of neighboring peoples. In addition, checks may be made on the veracity of one or the other by determining its reliability in reporting verified information. For instance, if the facts a history transmits can be consistently corroborated by other sources whenever they are available, then the history can probably be trusted to tell the truth in the instance when corroboration is not possible. The account should be accepted on its merits, Barnes says, and not judged by whether or not it has been written down. Unfortunately today, he laments, "no song-history is better than a fable unless it has been written by a dipper of a pen into a pot of ink."[14]

"The Old Bardic Poetry"[15] treats a similar subject; in fact, the introduction to this work summarizes some of his previous statements on the oral formulaic tradition in general and on Welsh prosody in particular. Some of the introductory remarks are new, however, and demonstrate his continuing interest in his subject. For example, he comments on the problem of determining the age of an unwritten poem or one recently written down by the age of particular words in the poem's vocabulary. He cites a case in which some previously unwritten songs composed in the old English speech of the Strongbow colony in the county of Wexford, Ireland, were taken down from the lips of an old man named Lett Sealy. A year later, a second version was written down, this from the voice of Toby Butler, another old man of the area. The versions were identical in most respects, but differed in the use of certain words: Sealy used the modern words "the," "when," and "each" while Butler used the older Forth words *a, fan,* and *earch.* The word-locks, or mnemonic devices, had done their work well, but could not prevent the intrusion of new words into the version as long as those words had the same meaning as the old and were of the same prosodic quantity. Thus, Barnes points out, dating a particular version of an orally transmitted text by dating the vocabulary can be very risky business indeed.

This piece is meant to be, however, an introduction to the work of the three great Celtic bards of ancient Britain: Llywarch Hen, Taliesin, and Aneurin. The first, Llywarch the Old, is depicted as a Celtic prince, one of the North British Cymri who have left their name in Cumberland. Llywarch was driven into Wales by the Saxons where, after a long life, he ended his days. Barnes refers to an old triad which identifies him as one of the three main counselors of King Arthur, but other triads are cited which make that claim unclear. Poems attributed to Llywarch the warrior are mostly on the subject of fighting, as one might expect, and specifically on battles between the Celts and the Saxons. One of these is on the death of Geraint, slain at the battle of Llongborth; Barnes takes this poem to be the British counterpart to the account of the battle of Portsmouth, found in the *Anglo-Saxon Chronicle.* After serving a sample of the poem through one of his own translations, Barnes comments on the verse form and then takes issue with Southey who, he says, has called Llyward's poetry rude: "Of severe form," Barnes says, but not rude.[16] He cites examples of Llywarch's work in the elegaic mode, two poems on the deaths of the Welsh princes Urien and Cynddylan, as well as poetry which presents proverbs. Barnes is interested, too, in some older verses of Llywarch which he describes as "folk-lore, or homely wisdom." Most of these, he says, connect a truth of matter or nature with a word of wisdom for man. He gives several examples, including the following:

Bright is the briar's bloom: no law hath need:

> From impure deeds withdraw; ·
> Ill manners are the greatest flaw.

The second clause of the first line carries a footnote, "Necessity hath no law." Obviously, Barnes approves of these "homely" rhymes which he compared to the Tuscan *stornelli;* he says that they provide a "verse blend" between a moral truth and a natural object. These bonds reinforced good thoughts as the ancient Briton carried on his daily pursuits in the fields and woodlands, his memory jarred to a moral teaching by the appearance of a gorse bloom or the twig of a birch tree. At least this, according to Barnes, was the idea. And naturally the school master turned clergyman who had written "homely rhymes" of his own would be favorably impressed by such verse. Taliesin and Aneurin, recognized by present-day scholars as the two premier Welsh poets, are also discussed. Barnes describes each as a true *penbierdd,* head-bard, or chief poet, and indicates that Taliesin, especially, is a metrical innovator.

Barnes's critical comments on the literature of his own day demonstrates the same erudition as do his works on literary history. In an article published in *Fraser's magazine* in 1863, he looks at the poetical work of Coventry Patmore.[17] He compares Patmore to Petrarch and Patmore's epic *Angel in the House* with Petrarch's *Rime.* Laura, as the ideal woman, Barnes says, is very much like Honoria, the heroine of *Angel* and a representative of what the Dorset poet calls the "high type" of womanhood. Both poets, he asserts, espouse the idea of the "majesty of pure-minded beauty as a refiner of man,"[18] even though he recognizes that many women might not agree. Patmore's poetry, Barnes seeks to show, picks up the tone of George Herbert's, even while it retains its own originality. This tone is recognizable in the "poetical surprises," which both poets show in their verse. The stance of Patmore's work is always decent and moral, thus deserving of our attention and praise. This is in indirect contrast, he says, to the "loose verses" of the Restoration period, many of which ridiculed women and marriage. He gives several examples, contrasting lines from Patmore to those of earlier verses.

In opting for Patmore's ideas—"good wisdom as well as good poetry"—Barnes compares them with those of other sages like Saadi, an old Pesian poet, who says that the poorest man becomes like a king when he marries a woman "buxom and godly."[19] Petrarch, he says, shares this idea as well, along with the Welsh bard Llywelyn Goch and the commentator of the Chinese *Book of Rewards*.

These comparisons and contrasts, extracted from a broad range of literary history, demonstrate how Barnes was able to draw upon his learning and make it apply to the subject at hand. His literary scholarship and criticism was often impressionistic, and sometimes even opinionated; but, without a doubt, its major tendency may be said to be instructive. In this lay its importance to his audience.

Chapter Six
Reputation and Influence
Contemporary Opinion

One of Barnes's most outspoken admirers during the poet's lifetime was Coventry Patmore, who compared the Dorset writer to Horace, Petrarch, Wordsworth, and Robert Burns. Patmore was himself a successful poet when he took up Barnes's cause in 1859. He had published the popular *The Angel in the House* in 1854, and, even though the poem was to be parodied by Swinburne and castigated by some critics, it established Patmore as a major literary figure in Victorian England. In addition to poetry, Patmore published literary essays and critical reviews in the leading periodicals of the day.

In 1859 Patmore reviewed *Hwomely Rhymes: A Second Collection of Poems in the Dorset Dialect;* in addition to the new Barnes edition, the 1859 *Burns Centenary Poems* was examined along with the 1847 edition of *Poems of Rural Life in the Dorset Dialect.* The review takes up fourteen pages of the *North British Review* for November—Patmore devotes a page and a half to Burns and the rest to the Dorset poet. While he notes that Barnes's poems are unpopular, counting it his "honour and pleasure of being probably the first to introduce the poetry of Mr. Barnes to the notice of the majority of our readers . . . ," Patmore recognizes that he is reviewing the work of "one of our very first poets."[1]

Barnes's insistence on using the dialect, he says, has probably a great deal to do with the lack of popularity, but in actual practice, Patmore insists, the language provides only minimal hindrance to the reader. The reviewer does ask the poet, however, to work on "popularizing his orthography" in order to remove "unnecessary limits" on a poetry which can be enjoyed by a wide audience. Another problem Patmore sees as causing lack of reader interest is the inclusion in the poetry volumes of "dry philological dissertation." These linguistic discussions detract from the poetry, he says, although he agrees with Barnes's contentions about the poetic superiority of the dialects of southwestern England.

Patmore's article gives several examples of the dialect poetry along with a commentary which expresses admiration for Barnes's accurate verse depiction of country life: "When Mr. Barnes represents rustic lovers, he does not put fine ladies into cotton gowns, and fine gentlemen into corduroy, and set them to talk modern sentiment in delicate phraseology; but he gives us the people themselves, with their rough and bold speech and manners, and the strong and simple current of their homely passions."[2] He also admires Barnes's humor and his gift for including those little touches, the attention to detail, which buoy up verisimilitude in literature.

A correspondence between Patmore and Barnes began with the admiring reviewer's letter to the Dorset poet in 1859. In this letter, Patmore asks, "May I take the liberty of saying that your poems have given me the most unmixed pleasure I have received from any poetry of our time?" And, he explains, "On reading Wordsworth and Burns I have often regretted the want in each of what the other possessed. I seem to find the spirits of the two united in a perfectly original way in your poems."[3] This high praise helped to start a friendship which was to last until Barnes's death. The two men exchanged letters, mostly on literary matters, and in 1863, after the death of his wife, Patmore made the first of several visits to the older poet's home in Dorset, accompanied by his daughter, Emily Honoria.

In 1862 Patmore published a literary essay entitled "William Barnes, the Dorsetshire Poet" in *Macmillan's Magazine*.[4] Like the earlier review, this essay opens with a discussion of the poet's lack of popularity. Here he cites three reasons, with the dialect and its attendant difficulties leading the list. The second problem he sees is that of the popular taste in literature; Barnes will immediately appeal only to the "perfectly unsophisticated in taste and the perfectly cultivated." His attractiveness does not extend to the great mass of readers, and thus, in terms of size of audience, he is relatively unpopular. The third reason, Patmore says, is that Barnes is "nothing but a poet. He does not there protest against anything in religion, politics, or the arrangements of society"; thus, he is not able to gain the automatic attention of any political faction or religious sect. Patmore adds: "nor has he the advantage of being able to demand the admiration of the sympathising public on the score that he is a chimney-sweep, or a rat-catcher, and has never learned to read."[5]

In his discussion of why Barnes merits the attention of the reading public, Patmore delivers some of his aesthetic theory, and indicates what he thinks a poet should be and what he should do:

The event which has occurred a thousand times, the moral truism, the scene in which *we* [Patmore's italics] can see little or nothing, because we have seen it so often—these are the themes which delight us most, and most justly, when, by the poet's help, we behold them as he, in his inspired moments, beholds them. . . . Sensible events and objects, then, manifested in their divine relations by the divine light, and expressed in verse, are poetry; and, whenever the poet enables us to see common and otherwise "commonplace" objects and events with a sense of uncommon reality and life, then we may be sure that this divine light is present.[6]

The ability of the poet to put the common into a new light is aided by the proper choice of both subject and language. This is done, Patmore says, by all the poets sometimes; Barnes follows this rule "with rare felicity and uniformity." This "freshness of feeling and perception" is at the heart of Barnes's poetry.

As we have seen from his letter to the Dorset poet, Patmore did not confine his praise to public utterances. He made sure that Hopkins was aware of Barnes's work by sending the former three volumes of Barnes's dialect poetry; he also commented favorably in letters to other literary friends. Patmore writes to Edmund Gosse, who had been introduced to Barnes by Thomas Hardy, "he has done a small thing well, while his contemporaries have been mostly engaged in doing big things ill."[7] To Dykes Campbell, Coleridge's biographer, he writes, "there is little 'form' in Herrick or William Barnes, but there is style—the true essential of poetry—very marked in each."[8]

He had laudatory things to say in his memoirs as well. There he maintains, "I am the only poet of this generation, except Barnes, who has steadily maintained a literary conscience."[9] Similarly, he says, "Not to run before he is sent is the first duty of a poet and that which all living poets—except Barnes—forget."[10]

For all his favorable commentary, though, Patmore does not lose his perspective. In an obituary piece published in the *Fortnightly Review* shortly after Barnes's death,[11] he calls the Dorset poet a classic, but a minor one. Patmore places his work with that of Herrick, Suckling, Burns, and Blake. Barnes's canon lacks that one great poem, the one that time will consider equivalent to Keats's

"Ode on a Grecian Urn" or Spenser's "Epithalamion," and that is why Patmore is reluctant to call him, after all, a poet of the first magnitude.

Gerard Manley Hopkins was another contemporary poet who admired Barnes. In his essay "Hopkins' Sprung Rhythm," Walter J. Ong includes a section which warns against the false starts possible in any study of Hopkins's prosody. A portion of this section deals with the relationship between Barnes and Hopkins, a relationship which, Ong says, "looks promising at first sight but goes little further in the way of explaining the connection of Hopkins' new rhythm with Old English."[12] Ong bases his statement on the fact that Hopkins had read little Barnes until very late—1885, in fact—citing a letter to Bridges in which Hopkins says he read only one of Barnes's poems prior to 1879, except for those he read as an undergraduate.[13] The extent of the impression made by those early readings is hard to judge, but we know that Hopkins was long an admirer of Barnes. As a matter of fact, in a letter to Patmore written in 1886, Hopkins says, "You are not to think I now begin to admire Barnes: I always did so, but it was long since I read him."[14]

Ong is right in asserting that a case can be made that the relationship between the two poets is based on appreciation more than influence. Hopkins admired Barnes for the simple reason that the Dorset poet was actively engaged in many of the intellectual pursuits that were of interest to Hopkins himself. These common pursuits included the study of Old English; the reintroduction of older words into the language and the subsequent use of these words in poetic diction; and the study of non-English language and literature, especially Welsh.

The first mention of Barnes that Hopkins makes is in the 1879 letter to Bridges mentioned above. He says that he disagrees with his correspondent's negative impression and that he is drawn to the use of dialect in the poetry. When used correctly, he says, the dialect displays the "spontaneousness" of the idea, and helps convince the reader that the poetry arises "from nature and not books and education." Hopkins says, too, that while the dialect may narrow Barnes's field, it "heightens his effect," resulting in a poetry which contains the very "instress" of the West country.[15]

Through the years, Hopkins remains appreciative of Barnes's poetry. In another letter to Bridges, the priest defends the Dorset poet, saying, "I hold your contemptuous opinion an unhappy mistake: he is a perfect artist and of a most spontaneous inspiration; it is as if Dorset life and Dorset landscape had taken flesh and tongue in the man."[16] Again, in a letter written a year later, he says, "You are quite wrong about Barnes' poems—not to admire them ever so much more." He goes on to tell Bridges that he had set two of the poems to music, testing the results with the aid of a pianist and two choristers. He continues to berate Bridges for his lack of enthusiasm in a subsequent letter where he praises Barnes for his "local colour."[17]

Hopkins praises Barnes in his correspondence with Patmore, too; in a letter written about the same time as the one to Bridges about setting the Dorset poems to music, Hopkins says

> I grant in Barnes an unusual independence and originality, due partly to his circumstances. It is his naturalness that strikes me most; he is like an embodiment or incarnation or manmuse of the country, of Dorset, of rustic life and humanity. He comes, like Homer and all poets of native epic, provided with epithets, images, and so on which seem to have been tested and digested for a long age in their native air and circumstances and to have a *keeping* which nothing else could give; but in fact they are rather all of his own finding and first throwing off. This seems to me very high praise. It is true they are not far-fetched or exquisite (I mean for instance his mentions of rooks or of brooks) but they are straight from nature and quite fresh. His rhythms are charming and most characteristic: these too smack of the soil.[18]

Hopkins does not allow his admiration to blind him, however. In the letter to Patmore, he says that he does not consider Barnes's use of *cynghanedd* to be quite successful. In fact, Hopkins says, he himself could do it better. In an earlier letter to Bridges, he allows that while Barnes is a fine poet—the Dorset dialect poems contain "more true poetry than in Burns"—his campaign for Saxonizing the language is hopeless. Hopkins cites the publication of Barnes's *An Outline of English Speechcraft,* a work, the Jesuit says, which is "written in an unknown tongue, a sort of modern Anglo Saxon, beyond all that Furnivall in all his wildest Forewords ever dreamed."[19]

Not that Hopkins disagrees with Barnes's intention. On the contrary, he says that he is saddened by the way in which the language has degenerated; "I weep to think what English might have been," he laments, and adds that he has found Old English to be much superior to the contemporary dialect. He, like Barnes, disapproves of the language's lack of purity. Unlike Barnes, however, Hopkins knows that it is unrealistic at best to expect the nation to return to a pure Teutonic tongue: "But the madness of an almost unknown man trying to do what the three estates of the realm together could never accomplish! He calls degrees of comparisons pitches of suchness: we ought to call them so, but alas!"[20]

Ong's discounting of the possibility of Barnes's influence on Hopkins is based primarily on two assertions. First, he says, Hopkins had only read Barnes's poems as an undergraduate, with the exception of one he had read in 1879. He goes on to say that subsequent readings of the Dorset poet occurred too late to influence the Jesuit's poetic techniques. This is true, of course, if one rejects the possibility of the influence of the undergraduate readings. As Hopkins was an undergraduate at Oxford during the period 1863–67, and as Hopkins's mature style was demonstrated for the first time in 1875 in "The Wreck of the *Deutschland*" (he wrote nothing significant between 1868 and 1875), it might be said that the reading of Barnes's poems came at a time when Hopkins's poetic ideas were being formulated. The Barnes poems could very well have had a profound yet consciously unrecognized influence on his mature poetic technique. Ong's second assertion is that Barnes's linguistic work could not have had an influence on Hopkins's diction since he did not read *An Outline of English Speech-Craft* until 1882. While this last is, of course, true, *Speech-Craft* is not the only volume in which Barnes puts forth his ideas on purifying English. His *Philological Grammar,* for example, came out in 1854, and Hopkins may have had occasion to look at any number of Barnes's subsequent publications, all of which preached the Saxon gospel.

While it is always difficult to make a case for or against the influence of one writer on another, the lack of hard evidence in the Hopkins–Barnes relationship makes it a particularly murky one. The case for appreciation is easily made, however, by the comments of Hopkins himself.

Thomas Hardy is another contemporary man of letters who admired the Dorset poet. Hardy, also a native of Dorset, knew Barnes personally from the time he was a schoolmaster in Dorchester. Barnes's school on South Street was next door to the architect's office in which Hardy worked as a young man. As a matter of fact, when the scholarly young architectural pupil got into one of his frequent linguistic or literary disputes with his master, John Hicks, and another pupil, he was sent next door to Barnes for the authoritative answer.[21] Years later, Hardy and Barnes were neighbors who often got together for walks in the countryside and for literary discussions. In 1883, Hardy brought Edmund Gosse to visit the elderly poet, the pair even staying to hear Barnes preach a sermon to his congregation. On one of Hardy's visits, Barnes treated him to an anecdote in which he recalled a visit of Louis Napoleon to Dorset. While Barnes and an acquaintance named Hann were walking together on a Sunday afternoon, they chanced to meet Louis Napoleon and his Dorchester host coming from the opposite direction. As the pairs met, Louis Napoleon, apparently on a whim, stuck his cane between Hann's legs and tripped him. The fiery Dorsetman leaped to his feet, according to Barnes, pulled off his coat, throwing it on his companion, and challenged Louis Napoleon to fight. Hann was cooled down, however, and the walk resumed, ending Barnes's only meeting with royalty.[22]

When Barnes died in 1886, Hardy walked from his home, Max Gate, to Winterbourn-Came Church to attend his friend's funeral. His poem "The Last Signal" alludes to this walk across the fields; as the coffin was being carried to the church, the sun glinted off some brass trimming on the coffin, reflecting in Hardy's eyes. The poet regarded this as a last gesture from a long-time friend.

Hardy also wrote an obituary notice for the *Athenaeum*,[23] which the *Dictionary of National Biography* used to gather details of Barnes's life. This tribute was later reprinted in *Life and Art,* a collection of essays by Hardy, and in other volumes.[24] The obituary contains the facts of Barnes's long life. But Hardy goes beyond this, including an examination of the poetry. Barnes, Hardy says, "when moved by the pervading instinct of the nineteenth century, . . . gives us whole poems of still life, unaffected and realistic as a Dutch picture. . . ."[25]

But Barnes is more than a landscape poet writing about the local countryside, Hardy says. "It is impossible to prophesy, but surely much English literature will be forgotten when 'Woak Hill' is still read for its intense pathos, 'Blackmore Maidens' for its blitheness, and 'In the Spring' for its Arcadian ecstasy."[26]

Hardy's praise, it seems, is genuine, for he paid Barnes the supreme compliment, that of emulation.[27] He uses Welsh techniques introduced into English by Barnes and, of course, makes use of the local dialect in both his prose and his poetry.

Modern Opinion

Earlier, Patmore called Barnes a literary "classic," defining his term as pertaining to a writer whom everyone claiming to be educated must read. If a writer is to remain a classic, he or she must stand the test of time; the writer's works must continue to be regarded as important enough to be read generations after they were written. Whether or not a piece of writing is read depends on literary taste, that commonality of mind that has the constancy of smoke. And taste, history tells us, is often given impetus in one direction or another by the pronouncements of the sages, the literary critics and commentators. The process is often two-directional as well; the comments of the critics in some cases reflect current literary taste, rather than direct it. In any event, an examination of critical statements on Barnes is helpful in determining what place he has held in the literary world in the years since his death.

In his 1939 essay, "William Barnes," for example, E. M. Forster indicates surprise that the Dorset poet has not been more "widely worshipped."[28] Forster's comments—more an appreciation than an analysis—show an admiration for the way in which Barnes seemed to heap up all the joy and beauty he could find in the world and present it to the reader.

He is appreciative, too, of Barnes's facility with poetic forms or his "poetic intelligence." He is amazed that a writer who celebrates the heart so much can still make such good use of his head. While he admits Barnes's idiosyncrasies, the question of popularity is a disturbing one to Forster because the Dorsetman wrote on subjects which move everyone in a way which everyone can understand. Thus, Forster cannot see why the public has neglected Barnes.

Others have agreed with Forster's observations. In 1950, Geoffrey Grigson anthologized many of Barnes's poems in a volume intended to introduce the poet to a modern audience.[29] His introductory essay is interesting because of the assessment of the poet's craftsmanship it offers as well as for Grigson's analysis of the poems. The attraction of Barnes's poetry, he says, lies in three things: the care with which Barnes selects, his sparseness, and the way he arouses emotion. Together, these make up his classicism, a term which Grigson uses to mean belonging to the Augustan tradition rather than to the romantic.

To Grigson Barnes's selection process involves not only subject matter and form, but language as well. He contends, unlike Hardy, that Barnes's use of dialect was calculated for effect and not done because of the poet's inability to express himself poetically in any language but that of his childhood. The dialect is seen as being an appropriate vehicle for the poetic subjects and characters in much the same way as the Doric dialect of Theocritus was for the *Idyllia*. Grigson also sees the subjects and characters as being chosen with care. The fact that Barnes's settings are nearly always the southwest of England does not mean that his poems are too narrow; this is avoided by a craftsmanlike variation in metrical forms and patterns which are chosen for their most harmonious effect. Much of Barnes's genius, then, lies in his ability to sift his materials for the authentic, the natural, and the beautiful.

The quality of sparseness, or "scarcity," as Grigson calls it, stems from Barnes's affinity for harmony or fitness. He points out that the poetry is seldom monotonous, never overworked, and is efficient in its effect. Barnes is always economical in his use of language, Grigson says, avoiding the verbosity of some contemporary poets, most notably John Clare. This sparseness, based on the sense of harmony, is a key element in the quality of classicism.

Harmony, too, is behind Barnes's quiet yet insistent emotion. He does not exhort his reader to strive or to seek, nor does he express the anxieties of the age; rather, his landscapes project calmly the interrelatedness of all things, the peaceful majesty of nature. Barnes is able, Grigson says, to paint this picture in many variations, each time with gentle emotion. He does not soar to the heights, but neither does he succumb to bathos; in this regard, too, Clare is offered as an example of what Barnes is not.

In Grigson's opinion then, these three elements—selection, scarcity or economy, and emotion—come together in Barnes to give his poetry a classical touch; they make up, the critic says, his "cool-aired quality."

Raynor Unwin's 1954 study of peasant poetry in England includes a section on Barnes because of the Dorsetman's obvious love and affinity for the rural working classes.[30] Unwin denies that Barnes is a passionate peasant-poet struggling for a place in the literary pantheon; rather, he is an educated, reserved artist working in the milieu he knew best. As such, he is recognized by Unwin as the classicist; at the same time, his care in observing the minute brings to mind the best of the Pre-Raphaelites, while Barnes's ability to relate the objects in nature to human emotion points to the poet's romantic tendencies.

Unwin sees that Barnes's central poetic theme is harmony—the interdependence of the men and women he knew with nature, of the earth with its inhabitants. In keeping with this theme is the tone of the poetry which is characterized by an aloof calmness. Barnes does not intrude personally into the poems, the critic says, yet there is always the air of empathy, the sense that through the poems, one is observing the passing parade of humanity against a simple, rustic background.

While Unwin appreciates Barnes's gift of expression, he realizes that it is a limited one. He comments on the impossibility of tracing a line of development in Barnes; the early resembles the late, and the poet's flame burned steadily if not spectacularly. The poems combine simplicity and dignity and depend upon a sincere love for humanity.

Placing William Barnes intellectually as well as chronologically in the center of the Victorian era, R. A. Forsyth in 1963 argues that Barnes's conservatism is a position come to as a result of dealing with the far-reaching changes of the nineteenth century.[31] In this endeavor, Barnes joins such other eminent Victorians as Matthew Arnold, Charles Kingsley, John Cardinal Newman, and John Stuart Mill. Barnes's achievement, Forsyth contends, lies in his forging of a myth out of the nineteenth-century Dorset countryside. This myth stands in opposition to the contemporary idea of progress which espoused the idea of the desirability of change and its inevitability. The myth resulted from Barnes's yearning to preserve the past and to provide what he considered to be valuable links between past and present forms of life in rural England.

In practice, Barnes seeks to do this by demonstrating that inhabitants of the past, even those living in primitive societies, are not inferior to moderns. The Welsh bards, for example, display artistic and intellectual skills which would be the envy of many nineteenth-century poets. Further, Barnes uses the poetic forms and meters of the past to show their effectiveness and immunity from time. His very language retains ties to the past which other dialects have relinquished, according to Forsyth. But most of all, Barnes's myth relies on his vision of an established order of nature which opposed the evolutionist idea of an emergent order. This scheme of things Barnes describes again and again, extolling harmony and stability while praising the inherent sanity of traditional country life. The presentation of this vision, carried out by his poetry, offers an alternative to the industrialization and urbanization which the proponents of progress saw as an inevitability.

In agreement with Forster and Grigson concerning Barnes's lack of popularity, Charles H. Sisson, also writing in the 1960s, says that the Dorsetman has been undervalued.[32] The poet offers more, he says, than mere regional interest or linguistic curiosity. He is a rural poet because he used the material at hand; his rural settings should not limit interest in his work any more than urban settings should limit the work of Baudelaire. Like all true poets, Sisson says, Barnes's vision goes beyond the "hwomely" aspects of his dramatic situations. This vision includes depicting the English countryside as an image of the natural order. This order is harmonious, its parts and inhabitants are cooperative, and it accounts for the past, present, and future as elements of natural growth. In presenting this order, Barnes avoids the extremes of overweening subjectivism and of mechanistic determinism; for Barnes, natural process includes growth and eventual decline of individual entities in the mortal world, but this world is only completed by the next. In the presentation of his world view, Sisson sees Barnes as being above mere politics. In the avoidance of contemporary issues for the sake of suggesting a more permanent order, Barnes is to be commended, rather than castigated or, worse, ignored.

Barnes's influence on that other Dorset literary figure, Thomas Hardy, is the subject of a recent study by Paul Zeitlow.[33] Zeitlow asserts that Barnes's poetry affected Hardy's in antithetical ways: the influence was both negative and positive. Zeitlow contends that Hardy took issue with the older man's world view, with the scenes and characters Barnes portrayed, and with the "dramatic truth" of some of the dialect poems. On the other hand, Hardy's admiration for Barnes can be demonstrated. He carried copies of Barnes's work around with him, quoted the poems in his own work, and published a selection of them. What the two poets share, Zeitlow says, is a reverence for places and things.

Another critic, Donald Wesling,[34] looks upon the Hardy–Barnes literary relationship in similar fashion. The novelist, he says, saw that Barnes's use of the dialect and other rural trappings acts as a "screen" to the uninitiated reader, causing much to be lost. Once

Hardy learned this "negative lesson" from the older poet, he was able to make the adjustment accordingly. He became highly selective in his own use of Dorset materials; an example is his attempt to combine dialect and standard speech as they related to social class. In this way, Wesling says, Hardy was able to go beyond Barnes's simple provincialism and to exploit the Dorset dialect, characters, and setting as background for his human drama.

Little had been done to examine Barnes's linguistic theories until the appearance of W. D. Jacobs's 1952 monograph.[35] Jacobs asserts that while poetry was Barnes's love, philology was his passion. And, he reasons, acclaim for the poetry should not preclude an appreciation of the philological works, although this seems to have been the case with most critics. He says that Barnes's linguistic contribution was a definite one; this contribution is worth study because the philologic theory was complemented with practice in Barnes's attempt to prove the practicality of native English. This "purist" approach to the language, Jacobs says, is behind the Dorsetman's claim to a place in linguistic history.

While he admits that some of Barnes's doctrine is trivial and cumbersome, Jacobs believes that the linguistics studies are interesting and valuable. Further, he thinks that resources of Saxon English which Barnes was attempting to make use of will in time be appreciated by the English-speaking world.

In the end, it must be said that Barnes is, as Patmore says, a minor classic. Modern critics agree with this assessment, for the most part, and agree that Barnes should be read by modern audiences. This assertion is based on three observations. First, the poet and his work played a part, albeit not a major one, in the literary and philological history of Victorian England. His work was known and praised by many of the major figures and, while the case for influence is rarely proved to everyone's satisfaction, the poems doubtless had an impact on their readers. Second, Barnes's interests and accomplishments were a microcosm of the main intellectual currents of the time. His poems reflect these interests and as such they stand as important documentary evidence for the study of nineteenth-century English society. Third, his poetry is valuable as poetry; the verse is rich, subtle, and written with true craftsmanship.

Notes and References

Chapter One

1. Thomas Hardy, "William Barnes: A Biographical Note," quoted in Lionel Johnson, *The Art of Thomas Hardy* (London: E. Matthews, 1894), p. 360.

2. Lucy E. Baxter, *The Life of William Barnes* (London, 1887), p. 24.

3. Baxter, *Life,* p. 24.

4. Denys Arthury Winstanley, *Early Victorian Cambridge* (Cambridge: at the University Press, 1940), p. 153. The intent of this degree originally was to encourage learning among the clergy who held no previous degree. Normally, candidates for the bachelor of divinity degree were required to hold the bachelor of arts and master of arts degrees. Students were not required to reside at Cambridge under the ten years' plan, although Barnes did spend the summers of 1847 and 1848 there.

5. The full title of Sir Charles Lyell's book is *Principles of Geology. Being an attempt to explain the former Changes of the Earth's Surface by reference to Causes now in Operation.* (London: J. Murray, 1830–32). The volume seeks to refute certain fundamentalist religious views which interpret literally the biblical accounts of the Creation. Robert Chambers's *Vestiges of the Natural History of Creation* (London: J. Churchill, 1844) puts forth the idea that organisms have a tendency to change in order to adapt themselves to their environment. Both books influenced Darwin and helped him formulate his famous hypothesis.

6. Baxter, *Life,* p. 110.

7. For a full discussion of this phenomenon, see Richard D. Altick, *The English Common Reader* (Chicago: University of Chicago Press, 1957), pp. 188 ff.

8. Ibid., p. 203.

9. Baxter, *Life,* p. 118.

10. Ibid., pp. 119–123. His daughter tells us that at the end of each day's entry of the diary Barnes wrote the single word "Giulia." This practice continued until his death.

11. Taliesin was one of the first major ancient Welsh poets. He wrote in the sixth century and established a tradition which survives until this day. For further information on this subject, see Robert Maynard Jones, *Highlights in Welsh Literature* (Swansea: C. Davies, 1969).

12. Baxter, *Life,* p. 261.
13. Quoted in ibid., p. 276.

Chapter Two

1. Lewis Mumford, *Technics and Civilization* (New York: Harcourt, Brace and Co., 1934), pp. 288–94.
2. John Heath-Stubbs, *The Darkling Plain* (London, 1950), p. 62.
3. James Whitcomb Riley, *The Letters of James Whitcomb Riley,* William Lyon Phelps, ed. (Indianapolis: Bobbs-Merrill Co., 1930), p. 179.
4. Preface to the 1800 edition of *The Lyrical Ballads.*
5. Hamlin Garland, *Crumbling Idols,* ed. Jane Johnson (Cambridge: Harvard University Press, Belknap Press, 1960).
6. *The Poems of William Barnes,* ed. Bernard Jones (Carbondale, 1962), p. 743; hereafter cited in the text as *P.*
7. Geoffrey Grigson, *Selected Poems of William Barnes* (London, 1950), p. 19.
8. Information on the publications of Barnes's poetry is based on Jones's forewords to the poems.
9. Grigson, *Selected Poems,* p. 10.
10. Ibid., p. 10.
11. Baxter, *Life,* p. 84.
12. Ibid., p. 84.
13. Grigson, *Selected Poems,* p. 12.
14. Forster, *Two Cheers for Democracy* (London, 1951), p. 198–91.
15. Thomas Carlyle, *Past and Present* (New York: Scribner, 1897), p. 196.
16. David Thomson, *England in the Nineteenth Century* (Baltimore: Penguin Books, 1950), p. 53.
17. Ibid., p. 54.
18. Ibid., p. 84.
19. *Macmillan's Magazine* 4 (1861):126.
20. Ibid., p. 127.
21. Ibid., p. 132.
22. Ibid.
23. Basil Taylor, *Constable: Paintings, Drawings, and Watercolours* (London: Phaidon, 1973).

Chapter Three

1. R. H. Robins, *A Short History of Linguistics* (Bloomington: University of Indiana Press, 1967), p. 116 and passim.
2. Hans Aarsleff, *The Study of Language in England, 1780–1860* (Princeton: Princeton University Press, 1967), p. 38 and passim.
3. Ibid., p. 161.

4. For further readings on this subject see Harrison Ross Steeves, *Learned Societies and English Literary Scholarship in Great Britain and the United States* (New York: Columbia University Press, 1913) and Murray, K. M. Elisabeth, *Caught in the Web of Words* (New Haven: Yale University Press, 1977).

5. Murray, *Caught in the Web of Words,* passim.

6. W. D. Jacobs, *William Barnes, Linguist* (Albuquerque, 1952), p. 9.

7. Quoted in ibid., p. 11.

8. *Early England and the Saxon English* (London, 1869), p. 101.

9. Baxter, *Life,* p. 206.

10. William Turner Levy, *William Barnes, The Man and the Poems* (Dorchester, 1960), pp. 5–6.

11. Quoted in Jacobs, *William Barnes,* p. 13.

12. Robins, *Short History,* p. 173.

13. Baxter, *Life,* p. 110.

14. Jacobs, *William Barnes,* p. 15.

15. Ibid.

16. *A Philological Grammar* (London, 1854), pp. v–vi; hereafter cited in the text as *PG.*

17. *Tiw* (London, 1862), p. xx.

18. Baxter, *Life,* p. 221.

19. *The Grammar and Glossary* (Berlin, 1863), p. 1.

20. Ibid., p. 9.

21. *An Outline of English Speechcraft* (London, 1878), p. iii; hereafter cited in the text as *O.*

22. Jacobs, *William Barnes,* p. 53.

Chapter Four

1. *Views of Labour and Gold* (London, 1859), p. 3; hereafter cited in the text as *V.*

2. See the Bibliography for specific titles and dates.

3. William Hone, *The Table Book of Daily Recreation and Information: Concerning Remarkable Men & Manners, Times & Seasons, Solemnities & Merrymakings, Antiquities & Novelties on the Plan of the Every-day book & Year Book, or Everlasting Calendar* (London: W. Tegg, 1832), pp. 1172, 1525, 1599.

4. "On the So-called Kimmeridge Coal Money," *Gentleman's Magazine,* February 1839.

5. *Notes on Ancient Britain and the Britons* (London, 1858), p. 3.

6. Ibid., p. 81.

7. Ibid., p. 105.

8. *Early England and the Saxon-English* (London, 1869), p. 4.

9. Ibid., p. 97.

10. "The Rise and Progress of Trial by Jury in Britain," *Macmillan's Magazine,* March 1862, pp. 412–20.

Chapter Five

1. "Thoughts on Beauty and Art," *Macmillan's Magazine,* May 1861, pp. 126–37.

2. Ibid., p. 127.

3. Baxter, *Life,* p. 60.

4. "Beauty and Art," p. 133.

5. Ibid., pp. 135–36.

6. Ibid., p. 130.

7. Baxter, *Life,* pp. 48–49.

8. Quoted in ibid., p. 43n.

9. *An Outline of Rede-Craft* (London, 1879), p. v; hereafter cited in the text as *RC.*

10. "The Rariora of Old Poetry," *Macmillan's,* May 1863.

11. "On the Credibility of Old Song-history and Tradition," *Fraser's Magazine,* September 1863, pp. 394–410.

12. Ibid., p. 394.

13. Ibid., p. 399.

14. Ibid., p. 400.

15. "The Old Bardic Poetry," *Macmillan's Magazine,* August 1867, pp. 306–17.

16. Ibid., p. 310.

17. "Patmore's Poems," *Fraser's Magazine,* July 1863, pp. 130–34.

18. Ibid., p. 131.

19. Ibid., p. 133.

Chapter Six

1. Coventry Patmore, "New Poems," *North British Review,* November 1859, pp. 339–52.

2. Ibid., p. 346.

3. Basil Champneys, *The Memoirs and Correspondence of Coventry Patmore* (London: G. Bell & Sons, 1900), p. 341.

4. Coventry Patmore, "William Barnes," *Macmillan's,* June 1862, pp. 154–63.

5. Ibid., p. 155.

6. Ibid., p. 156.

7. Patmore to Gosse, 6 September 1886, in Champneys, *Memoirs,* p. 348.

8. Patmore to Campbell, 7 May 1888, in ibid., p. 362.

9. See ibid., p. 261.

10. Ibid., p. 254.

11. Coventry Patmore, "An English Classic, William Barnes," *Fortnightly Review,* November 1886, pp. 659–70.

12. Norman Weyand, S.J., ed., *Immortal Diamond: Studies in Gerard Manley Hopkins* (New York: Sheed & Ward, 1949), p. 96.

13. C. C. Abbott, ed., *The Letters of G. M. Hopkins to Robert Bridges* (Oxford: Oxford University Press, 1955), pp. 87–88.

14. C. C. Abbott, ed., *The Further Letters of G. M. Hopkins* (London: Oxford University Press, 1956), p. 370.

15. Abbott, *Letters,* p. 88.

16. Ibid., p. 221.

17. Ibid., p. 236.

18. Abbott, *Further Letters,* pp. 370–71.

19. Abbott, *Letters,* p. 162.

20. Ibid.

21. Florence Emily Hardy, *The Early Life of Thomas Hardy* (New York: Macmillan and Co., 1928), p. 37.

22. Ibid., pp. 229–30.

23. *Athenaeum,* 16 October 1886.

24. Ernest Brennecke, Jr., ed., *Life and Art* (New York: Greenberg, 1925), pp. 53–55.

25. Ibid., p. 53.

26. Ibid., p. 54.

27. J. O. Bailey, *The Poetry of Thomas Hardy* (Chapel Hill: University of North Carolina Press, 1970), pp. 376–77.

28. E. M. Forster, "William Barnes," in *Two Cheers for Democracy* (New York, 1951), pp. 197–200.

29. Grigson, *Selected Poems,* pp. 1–30.

30. Raynor Unwin, "The Language of Speech: Relph and Barnes," in *The Rural Muse* (London, 1954), pp. 143–64.

31. R. A. Forsyth, "The Conserving Myth of William Barnes," *Victorian Studies* 6 (June 1963):325–34.

32. Charles H. Sisson, "William Barnes," in *Art and Action* (London, 1965), pp. 30–46.

33. Paul Zeitlow, "Thomas Hardy and William Barnes: Two Dorset Poets," *PMLA* 84, no. 2 (March 1969):291–303.

34. Donald Wesling, "Hardy, Barnes, and the Provincial," *Victorian Newsletter* 55 (Spring 1979):18–19.

35. See chapter 3, note 6.

Selected Bibliography

PRIMARY SOURCES

1. Poetry

Orra, a Lapland Tale. Dorchester: I. Clark, 1822.

Poems in the Dorset Dialect. London: J. Russell Smith, 1844.

Poems, Partly of Rural Life in National English. London: J. Russell Smith, 1846.

Hwomely Rhymes. London: J. Russell Smith, 1850.

Third Collection of Poems in Dorset Dialect. London: J. Russell Smith, 1863.

Poems of Rural Life in Common English. London: Macmillan, 1868.

Poems of Rural Life in the Dorset Dialect. London: Kegan Paul & Co., 1879.

2. Modern Collections and Selections of Poetry

Select Poems of William Barnes. Edited by Thomas Hardy. London: Henry Frowde, 1908. The introductory comments are laudatory, yet accurate.

Twenty Poems in Common English by William Barnes. Edited by John Drinkwater. Oxford: Basil Blackwell, 1925. Includes introduction.

Poems Grave and Gay by William Barnes. Edited by Giles Dugdale. Dorchester: Longmans, 1949. Includes a foreword and biographical notes.

Selected Poems of William Barnes. Edited by Geoffrey Grigson. London: Routledge & Kegan Paul, 1950. The best selection, in that the poems included are representative of the corpus. The introduction is insightful and helpful.

A Fadge of Barnes. Edited by J. Stevens Cox. Dorset: Beaminster, 1956. Verse and prose pieces contributed by Barnes to *The Hawk* in 1867. Contains two previously unpublished letters from Barnes to James Allen.

The Poems of William Barnes. Edited by Bernard Jones. 2 vols. Carbondale: Southern Illinois University Press, 1963. This is the collected edition of the poems. It includes an excellent introduction, a good set of textual notes, and a helpful glossary of the Dorset dialect.

154

William Barnes: A Selection of His Poems. Edited by Robert Nye. Oxford: Fyfield Books, 1972. A good introductory volume to the poet's work.

3. Prose Works

The Etymological Glossary. London: Whittaker, Teacher, & Arnot, 1829.

A Catechism of Government in General, and of England in Particular. Shaftesbury: Bastable, 1833.

A Few Words on the Advantages of a More Common Adoption of the Mathematics as a Branch of Education. London: Whittaker & Co., 1834.

A Mathematical Investigation of the Principle of Hanging Doors, Gates, Swing Bridges, and Other Heavy Bodies. Dorchester: Simmonds & Sydenham, 1835.

An Investigation of the Laws of Case in Language. London: Whittaker & Co., 1840.

An Arithmetical and Commercial Dictionary. London: Whittaker & Co., 1841.

The Elements of Grammar. London: Longmans & Co., 1842.

Exercises in Practical Science. Dorchester: Clark, 1844.

Outlines of Geography and Ethnography for Youth. Dorchester: Barclay, Cornhill, 1847.

Se Gefylsta: An Anglo-Saxon Delectus. London: J. Russell Smith, 1846.

A Philological Grammar. London: J. Russell Smith, 1854.

Notes on Britain and the Ancient Britons. London: J. Russell Smith, 1858.

Views of Labour and Gold. London: J. Russell Smith, 1859.

Tiw, or a View of the Roots and Stems of the English as a Teutonic Tongue. London: J. Russell Smith, 1862.

A Grammar and Glossary of the Dorset Dialect. Berlin: Philological Society, 1863.

Early England and the Saxon English. London: J. Russell Smith, 1869.

An Outline of English Speechcraft. London: Kegan Paul & Co., 1878.

An Outline of Redecraft, or Logic. London: Kegan Paul & Co., 1879.

4. Contributions to Periodicals

"On English Derivatives." *Gentleman's Magazine,* June 1831.

"On the Structure of Dictionaries." *Gentleman's Magazine,* August 1831.

"Pronunciation of Latin." *Gentleman's Magazine,* October 1831.

"Hieroglyphics." *Gentleman's Magazine,* December 1831.

"Napper's Mite, Dorchester." *Gentleman's Magazine,* May 1833.

"Silton Church." *Gentleman's Magazine,* June 1833.

"Sturminster Newton Church." *Gentleman's Magazine,* June 1833.

"The English Language." *Gentleman's Magazine,* June 1833.

"Nailsea Church, Somerset." *Gentleman's Magazine,* July 1833.

"Chelvey, Somerset." *Gentleman's Magazine*, September 1833.
"Puncknowle Church." *Gentleman's Magazine*, July 1835.
"On Roman Numerals." *Gentleman's Magazine*, December 1837.
"On Aesop." *Gentleman's Magazine*, June 1838.
"Some Etymologies." *Gentleman's Magazine*, July 1838.
"On the So-called Kimmeridge Coal Money." *Gentleman's Magazine*, February 1839.
"Battle of Pen." *Gentleman's Magazine*, February 1839.
"The Roman Amphitheatre, Dorchester." *Gentleman's Magazine*, May 1839.
"The Hindoo Shasters." *Gentleman's Magazine*, June 1839.
"The Phoenicians." *Gentleman's Magazine*, August 1839.
"Hindoo Pooran and Sciences." *Gentleman's Magazine*, September 1839.
"Hindoo Fakeers." *Gentleman's Magazine*, January 1840.
"Dorset Dialect Compared with Anglo-Saxon." *Gentleman's Magazine*, January 1840.
"The Old Judge's House, Dorchester." *Gentleman's Magazine*, November 1840.
"Education in Words and Things." *Gentleman's Magazine*, January 1841.
"Fielding's House at Stour." *Gentleman's Magazine*, February 1841.
"Goths and Teutons." *Gentleman's Magazine*, May 1841.
"Laws of Case." *Gentleman's Magazine*, May 1841.
"The Beautiful in Nature and Art." *Macmillan's*, May 1861.
"The Rise and Progress of Trial by Jury in Britain." *Macmillan's*, March 1862.
"The Rariora of Old Poetry." *Macmillan's*, May 1863.
"On the Credulity of Old Song, History, and Tradition." *Fraser's Magazine*, September 1863.
"Plagiarism." *Macmillan's*, November 1866.
"On Bardic Poetry." *Macmillan's*, August 1867.

SECONDARY SOURCES

1. Biographies

Baxter, Lucy. *The Life of William Barnes.* London: Macmillan, 1887. The standard biography. All other accounts of the poet's life rely heavily on this work written by his daughter.
Dugdale, Giles. *William Barnes of Dorset.* London: Cassell, 1953. This is the only modern biography of the poet.

2. Criticism

Badham-Thornhill, Desmond. *William Barnes of Dorset.* Beaminster: J. S. Cox, 1964. A nineteen-page booklet on the poet and his work.

Forster, E. M. "William Barnes." In *Two Cheers for Democracy.* London: E. Arnold, 1951, pp. 197–200. Short, favorable comment—mostly generalities.

Forsyth, R. A. "The Conserving Myth of William Barnes." *Victorian Studies* 6 (1963):325–34. An excellent discussion of Barnes's attempts to preserve the Germanic elements in the language and what was best from the past.

Grigson, Geoffrey. *The Harp of Aeolus.* London: Routledge & Kegan Paul, 1947. A brief mention of Barnes's work in this volume.

———. *Poems and Poets.* London: Macmillan, 1969. Barnes is used to illustrate one of the lectures in this collection.

Hardy, Thomas. "The Rev. William Barnes, B.D." *Athenaeum,* 16 October 1886, pp. 501–2. An obituary in which Hardy says, "he gives us whole poems of still life, unaffected and realistic as a Dutch picture."

Hearl, Trevor W. *William Barnes: The Schoolmaster.* Dorset: Longmans, 1966. Discusses Barnes's educational theories and practices.

Heath-Stubbs, John. *The Darkling Plain.* London: Eyre & Spottiswoode, 1950. Discusses Barnes—along with John Clare and Robert Stephen Hawker—as a regionalist poet.

Hinchy, F. S. *The Dorset William Barnes.* Blandford, Dorset: F. S. & V. M. Hinchy, 1966. A discussion of Barnes's poetry and life, with emphasis on the latter, from an enthusiast's viewpoint.

Jacobs, W. D. *William Barnes, Linguist.* University of New Mexico Publications in Language and Literature, no. 9. Albuquerque: University of New Mexico Press, 1952. An intelligent discussion of Barnes's linguistic efforts. Heavily in favor of Barnes's "Saxonizing" efforts.

Larkin, Philip. "William Barnes." *Listener,* 16 August 1962. A brief appreciation.

Levy, William Turner. *William Barnes: The Man and the Poems.* Dorchester: Longmans, 1960. A well-documented survey of Barnes's poetry and linguistic ideas.

Patmore, Coventry. "William Barnes, the Dorsetshire Poet." *Macmillan's,* June 1862, pp. 155–63. A thoughtful examination of Barnes's poetry. Asserts that the poet treats the commonplace with a "Sense of uncommon reality and life."

———. "An English Classic, William Barnes." *Fortnightly Review,*

November 1886, pp. 659–70. Memorial piece in which Patmore tries to establish Barnes as "a minor classic" along with Burns.

Sisson, Charles H. "William Barnes." In *Art and Action*. London: Methuen, 1965, pp. 30–46. Sisson sees Barnes as transcending contemporary issues and as presenting a vision of natural order in the world.

Unwin, Raynor. *The Rural Muse*. London: George Allen & Unwin, 1954. Barnes is discussed in a section of the "language of speech" in which he tries to place the work of the poet within the context of other rural poets of the eighteenth and nineteenth centuries.

Wesling, Donald. "Hardy, Barnes, and the Provincial." *Victorian Newsletter* 55 (Spring 1979):18–19. The uses to which each of the poets put the language and descriptions of Dorsetshire are discussed.

Zeitlow, Paul. "Thomas Hardy and William Barnes: Two Dorset Poets." *PMLA* 84, no. 2 (March 1969):291–303. A useful discussion of the literary relationship of the two friends.

Index

821.8
B261

116 673